BRYAN FOSTER

CHURCH MARKETING MANUAL

for the

Digital Age

2nd edition

Attempts have been made to contact copyright holders or to abide by all the Terms and Conditions associated with copyright available on each website. If there are any errors or omissions, copyright holders are asked to contact Great Developments Pty Ltd so that acknowledgements or adjustments can be updated. Other companies wishing to be included in the next edition should contact the publisher.

Published in Australia in 2011
by Great Developments Pty Ltd
20 Aldrin Avenue
Benowa, Gold Coast, Queensland, Australia 4217
ABN: 13133435168
USA: EIN 98-0689457
http://churchparishmarketing.com

1st Edition   published 2009 as Church Parish Marketing e-Handbook: Easy to Use Guide to Market Your Church Parish Deanery
2nd Edition   published 2010 as Church Marketing Manual for the Digital Age (2nd ed) e-book
                     published 2011 as Church Marketing Manual for the Digital Age (2nd ed) paperback

Paperback edition printed by CreateSpace, part of the Amazon group of companies, USA.

National Library of Australia Cataloguing-in-Publication entry

Author: Foster, Bryan, 1957-
Title: Church marketing manual for the digital age / Bryan Foster.
Edition: 2nd ed.
ISBN: 9780980610765 (pbk.)
Series: Marketing manuals for the digital age.
Notes: Includes bibliographical references and index
Subjects: Parishes--Marketing.
                     Clergy--Office—Marketing
Dewey Number: 254.3

ISBN: 0980610761
ISBN-13: 9780980610765

BRYAN FOSTER

CHURCH MARKETING MANUAL

for the

Digital Age

2nd edition

Table of Contents

About the Author

Bryan Foster comes with over twenty years of leadership and marketing experience in Catholic parishes, deanery and schools. He has marketed the Catholic parish and school in both the city and country. A wealth of church marketing strategies, examples and samples has been developed.

He is presently the Director of his company, Great Developments Pty Ltd – an internet publishing company, which specializes in books and e-books for marketing churches and schools. He continues his active association with the local Catholic parish and also teaches in the local Catholic secondary school.

Bryan has been the:

- South Coast Deanery Pastoral Council, Chair
- St Mary's Parish Pastoral Council, Coomera, Chair
- Surfers Paradise Parish Pastoral Council, Surfers Paradise, Secretary
- St Kevin's School, Parents and Friends Association, Benowa, President
- St Joseph's, Tara, Principal
- St Mary's, Goondiwindi, Principal
- Aquinas College, Southport, Assistant Principal RE and Marketing Manager.

Most of these are on the Gold Coast, Queensland, Australia.

He has also been a Catching Fire: Evangelization and Spiritual Formation, Education Officer, Brisbane Catholic Education, Brisbane.

Bryan holds a Master of Education (Religious Education) degree.

A highly ethical approach to marketing, and passion for marketing the Church, Catholic schools and his company, was formed as a result of his extensive Catholic school and Religious Education leadership, marketing and teaching experience.

He has assisted many school and parish marketing managers.

Bryan has taught for over 30 years in Catholic schools from Years 1 to 12. He has held various senior and middle management positions: a primary school Principal in two schools, Assistant Principal RE in secondary school, Years 9, 11 and 12 Coordinator, various Acting Assistant Principal positions and School Marketing Manager.

He holds a:

- Master of Education from the Australian Catholic University in Sydney
- Bachelor of Education}
- Graduate Diploma in Religious Education}
- Diploma of Teaching} from McAuley Teachers College in Brisbane
- Diploma of Religious Education from the Institute of Faith Education, Brisbane.

His wife, eldest daughter and son all teach in Catholic primary schools, while his younger daughter attends a Catholic secondary school.

Testimonials

"Bryan possesses outstanding skills in marketing, advertising and communication. His natural aptitude for leadership, his great love for education and his engaging manner with people of all ages equipped him for success in Public Relations and Promotions."

– Nancy Freddi rsm, Congregation Vicar, Sisters of Mercy, Melbourne, Australia.

"I find Bryan Foster's new book will help considerably with marketing our Catholic parishes in the modern world. I am especially drawn to the chapters on Parish – School relationships and the uses of the internet, in particular the parish website.

The *Church Marketing Manual for the Digital Age (2nd ed)*, will be a highly valued resource within the Surfers Paradise Parish. "

– Fr Dan Ryan PP – Sacred Heart Parish, Surfers Paradise

"...the book has much to offer to help parishes to promote themselves...

Bryan Foster's *Church Marketing Manual for the Digital Age (2nd ed)*, provides a useful model for making better known what a parish has to offer, and connecting with people who have not yet become registered parishioners, and the wider community in general.

Bryan's book comes as a result of many years of parish and school involvement, and so he is aware of some of the unique issues that parishes face, especially with limited personnel and finances. "

– Fr Adrian Sharp PP - St Mary's Parish, Coomera, Gold Coast

The *Church Marketing Manual for the Digital Age (2nd ed)* by Bryan Foster, I believe, holds the key to improving many of our parish communication mediums. From relationships with our schools to communicating with our parishioners through to web design and blogs, this book gives strategies for growth opportunities within our parish.

I would highly recommend this book to other parishes as a tool which could be used in groups or by the Parish Priest or Parish Administrator."

– Sonya Slayter, Parish Administrator - Surfers Paradise Parish

Acknowledgements

A successful Church Marketing Plan is only possible with the support of the key stakeholders within the Church. I would truly like to offer my sincere thanks to a most remarkable group of people from both the Church and school settings who have both supported and inspired me over many years. There has been a very significant priestly and religious influence. This list appears exhaustive but unfortunately I realize that I have no doubt missed someone, my sincerest apologies and thanks.

Particular thanks must go to Archbishop John Bathersby, Archbishop of Brisbane; the late Archbishop Francis Rush, Archbishop of Brisbane; Bishop Bill Morris, Bishop of Toowoomba and former Parish Priest of Surfers Paradise; Bishop Michael Putney, Bishop of Townsville; the late Fr Bernie O'Shea, former Director Brisbane Catholic Education and Parish Priest Dutton Park Brisbane; Fr Keith Turnbull, retired and former Parish Priest Southport; Fr Peter Dillon, Dean of the South Coast and Parish Priest Southport, former Administrator of St Stephen's Cathedral and Director of Centacare, Brisbane; Fr Kevin Carey, former Dean of the South Coast; Fr Patrick Malony, Parish Priest Burleigh Heads and former Dean of the South Coast; Fr Michael McCarthy, Rector Holy Spirit Seminary Banyo and former Parish Priest Surfers Paradise; Fr Dan Ryan, Parish Priest Surfers Paradise; Fr Gerry Hefferan, former Parish Priest of St Mary's Coomera; Fr Ken Howell, Dean Central Brisbane, Administrator of St Stephen's Cathedral, Vice Rector Holy Spirit Seminary Banyo and former Associate Pastor at Burleigh Heads; Fr Michael Carroll, retired and former Parish Priest of St Mary's Goondiwindi,; Fr John Quinlan, former Parish Priest Tara; Fr Alan Gibson former Associate Pastor at Southport; Fr Adrian Sharp, Parish Priest Coomera; Fr Paul Chandler, Associate Pastor at St Stephen's Cathedral, Brisbane and former Associate Pastor at Southport; former priests Peter Ryan, Leo Simonis and Stephen Byrne.

To the Christian Brothers and staff who taught me at Aquinas College, the Sisters of Mercy and other lecturers of McAuley College Brisbane and Australian Catholic University Sydney, especially Sr Kath Burke and Sr Narelle McCoy.

Along with the communities of St Bernard's School Brisbane, Seton College Brisbane, St Mary's School Goondiwindi, St Joseph's School Tara, Corpus Christi College Brisbane and Marymount College Gold Coast, my special thanks for being initiators in my marketing formation.

To the staff, parents, students and priests of Aquinas College, Gold Coast, your support, encouragement and ideas have been instrumental in developing the College's successful School Marketing Plan over all the years since 1994.

To the Aquinas College Principals over those years of marketing the College, Mr. Terry Enright, Sr Nancy Freddi rsm and Mrs. Maryanne Finder, a particular special mention and thanks for supporting the Aquinas College Marketing Plan and Manager over all these years.

I would also like to acknowledge two very key people I worked and celebrated sacramentally with over the past 10+ years: Sr Moira Broderick, Pastoral Associate and Fr Gerry Hefferan former Parish Priest at my parish of St Mary's at Coomera on the Gold Coast.

These past few years I had a unique and wonderfully enriching experience through having my first true Spiritual Director, Br Bill Tarrant, a Marist Brother. We both worked with an inspirational Jill Gowdie as part of the Catching Fire: Evangelization and Spiritual Formation Team at Brisbane Catholic Education Office in 2008.

Finally a warm-hearted and special thanks to my wife, Karen, and three children, Leigh-Maree, Andrew and Jacqueline, along with my parents, Frank and Mary, and other family members, who have supported and encouraged me in this role over so many years. Your love has always been so necessary for the success.

Preface

The development of two key resources – the *CPM: Church Parish Marketing* interactive website and the *Church Marketing Manual for the Digital Age (2nd ed), (2011)* paperback, came about out of the need for quality, easy to use resources for marketing churches, parishes and deaneries, in what is a very commercially orientated society - a society which is highly in need of the Church's message.

The Church community needs to use all appropriately available resources to get the Church's message to as many people as possible in effective, attractive and enjoyable ways. This new *Church Marketing Manual for the Digital Age* (2011) is the 2nd edition of the popular *Church Parish Marketing e-Handbook: Easy to Use Guide to Market Your Church Parish Deanery* (published 2009).

Feedback resulting from the original CPM website, which has been continually developed since its inception, would suggest that this website, which houses the e-book version of this paperback, plays an important part in marketing the church, parish and deanery for a growing group of like-minded people.

The CPM website at http://churchparishmarketing.com/ has an array of interactive components, which would assist with the marketing of your church / parish. Two popular interactive aspects are the *Blogs* and the *Hints and Tips*. These are regularly updated. Readers are encouraged to offer their own thoughts publicly through the Blogs or privately to the author through the Contact Us.

If you would like to receive RSS feeds of any of the webpage updates e.g. *Blogs, Hints and Tips, Specials* and *News,* just click on the RSS orange symbol, which is either on the webpage or above on the toolbar, and follow the instructions. RSS feeds update you once something new is added to each selected webpage. (More on RSS is found in the book.)

Throughout the book the terms 'church' and 'parish' are interchangeable? Depending on the various experiences of the readers, these terms are often synonymous. For simplicity in this text, these terms will be interchanged with both referring to 'the People of God in a particular community.'

Introduction

The *Church Marketing Manual for the Digital Age (2nd ed)* (2011) contains a major digital section for marketing churches in the modern age – over 80 pages. Over 70 screenshots of actual internet pages are included to assist. The other contemporary marketing methods have also been updated. A combination of the digital and other contemporary and traditional methods is critical for a successful church marketing plan. This text begins with a sample church marketing plan overview and concludes with an invitation to begin creating your Church Marketing Action Plan on the pages provided.

For those who have purchased the church marketing e-book from the CPM website and opened it on your computer, with your internet connection on, you will be able to link directly from the e-book to various websites – over 100 website links are included. As an example, if you hold down the Control key and do a left click while hovering over the blue link e-Book you will go directly to the webpage describing in detail the new *Church Marketing Manual for the Digital Age (2nd ed)* e-book. Otherwise, just copy the link from the book and place it in the url / domain bar and hit enter.

The screenshot images taken directly of various websites, form part of this instruction manual, to assist you with seeing what various sites offer. These also show what you would see if you progressed with using these sites, or becoming a member of those sites with certain membership privileges. These memberships are mostly free of charge.

This book has an easy to use approach. It is written in clear, concise, summarized, point form, which engages and motivates the reader.

Step-by-step suggestions and instructions enable the Church Marketing Manager (CMM) to work toward the implementation of the Church Marketing Plan in the best way the CMM feels possible within his / her context.

This book aims to take away most of the trepidation various readers may feel about certain aspects of marketing. Apart from the digital age challenges, which have been simply explained, another common challenge is dealing with the traditional mass media. This challenge is addressed through explaining how best to use the media to the church's advantage, as well as how best to market the parish through the media. Another is the challenge to effectively work through the production of various marketing resources. These are covered throughout the book.

Church Marketing Plan

Preparing an effective, efficient and creative Church Marketing Plan is essential for success:

1. This book begins with a Sample OVERVIEW of a Church Marketing Plan.

2. Each aspect of this Plan is dealt with in considerable detail throughout the Manual.

3. Your Action Plan is then called for at the end of the text.

Church Parish Marketing (CPM)

Website

The *CPM: Church Parish Marketing* website aims to continually engage the reader as the website grows and develops according to the needs of those interested in this interactive site.

Free membership of the site offers the opportunity to be fully informed as new developments occur. To join the CPM website just hold down the control key and click on *Join Now* or go to http://churchparishmarketing.com/member-login .

The website contains the e-book *Church Marketing Manual for the Digital Age (2nd ed)* in the *Online Shop* plus regularly updated: *Blogs, Hints and Tips* and *News* items.

Interactive contact may be made through the *Blogs* or *Contact Us*.

The e-book overview is detailed at *e-Books*, detail on the author is at *Bryan Foster*, and there are pages on *Testimonials* and *Sponsorship,* etc.

There are also a *Gallery* of Photos and a gallery of *Videos,* as well as the *Site Search* option on each page.

Many screenshots have been taken from this CPM website and my private social networking sites, etc., and used in the 'Church Marketing - Internet Applications...' chapter. These are used to help clarify various aspects to do with websites, the internet and all that both offer and are not used to what may appear as self-promotion. This concentration on just key websites occurred due to the difficulty of gaining copyright permission from a larger number of websites.

Church Marketing Plan Overview

Church Marketing Plan Overview Sample

Define what you have to offer:
- vision and mission, personnel, sacramental / prayer life, pastoral and welfare support programs, schools, religious and pastoral education, facilities, etc
- specific ages and groups catered for - from infants to the elderly
- future plans – programs, staffing, facilities, etc

Define your target group:
- through surveys, observations, experience, gifts and talents available / needed
- proximity to / involvement with church and educational institutes – elementary / primary, secondary and tertiary
- any expansion – programs, facilities, staffing

Budget:
- realistically support the church marketing plan
- be flexible and open to growth and change as the needs arise
- continually develop over time through needs and experiences

Personnel and Talents available - including Church Marketing Manager

Select Marketing Strategies:
- Church Marketing Relationships
- Church Marketing Resources (including branding, advertising)
- Using the Media
    * Internet and other Contemporary methods
    * Both for Free (Media Releases / Editorial, etc) and for Fee (Advertising)

Evaluation

Church Marketing
Internet Applications
incl.
Samples and Instructions

Church Marketing Internet Applications including Samples and Instructions

The internet provides so many church marketing opportunities that are:

- very contemporary
- popular with a significant and ever-increasing number of our church community
- ever-growing in possibilities
- often inexpensive or free
- fun!

The modern church and parish needs to be actively involved with many of these internet opportunities, otherwise they will unnecessarily fall behind the interest level and communication methods of an ever-growing number of our parishioners – with what could be serious ramifications for all concerned.

The CHALLENGE has been issued!

Headings

Website
Website Management Software Sample
RSS Feeds
SEOs
Blogs
Emails
e/i-Newsletters and e/i-Flyers
Social Networking Websites
Video Uploads
Chat Rooms
Skype

Website

The church / parish website is becoming one of the most important forms of marketing the parish. It is often where parish information is initially found.

The website is often one of the first places that potential families and parishioners get an overall feel and basic appreciation of the potential for their involvement in parish life.

Creating a Website - Background

Investigation in this area is critical.

The church will need expertise to create and then continually update a good website.

The initial construction of the website may come from parish staff, IT skilled parishioners, school IT staff or from outside consultants.

The continual updating would best be done within the parish. In-servicing staff for making these updates would be money well spent.

An option, I have found very beneficial, follows.

Management Software

Another option is to have the website embedded in to management software which allows for management of the site. This takes the site beyond the static and into the realm of continual fluid development – Web 2.0.

The expense of this option is not considerable and with negotiation within the field a reasonable monthly cost would be expected. I would suggest speaking with trusted others in deciding on the businesses offering this support. (See 'Website Management Software Sample' in this chapter for a specific example.)

This software allows for various detailed reports of website usage. It could include:

- the whereabouts in the world of visitors to your site
- number of webpages they visited
- the content viewed from webpages and applications they visited
- where they entered and exited the website
- who is exploring your site, through IP (Internet Protocol) addresses
- the browsers they used to link to your website
- any commercial activities you may have as part of your website, etc.

This allows for the non-IT expert to update the website regularly, from uploading photos, literature items, to adding webpages, blogs, galleries of photos and videos, etc.

There are numerous other capacities depending on the management software.

Always Interactive supplies my management software. Three such samples of my website's details are included and shown below at: http://www.alwaysinteractive.com/

Reproduction of all 'Always Interactive' web-screens in this e-book reproduced with permission of Always Interactive at http://www.alwaysinteractive.com/.

Geographic Locations and Viewing Numbers

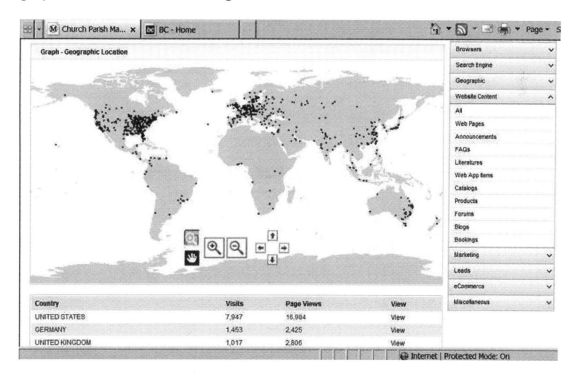

Webpages Viewed and Numbers per Page

Location, Visits and Page Views, New and Returning Visits and Top Sources

The CPM: Church Parish Marketing website http://churchparishmarketing.com created in January 2009 developed well over the year. Below is a summary of that growth as displayed through the management software provided by http://www.alwaysinteractive.com/.

Target Audiences

The website is also where more and more parishioners will continually visit throughout their time in the parish.

Parish Marketing Managers and key parish staff should use the website for interaction between the various stakeholders within the parish e.g. their parishioners, potential parishioners, staff, schools and groups within the parish.

Regularly updated bulletin boards and newsletters, upcoming liturgical and social events, St Vincent de Paul and other charitable needs and requests, photo and video galleries of parish activities, etc are needed.

To view good church websites, for ideas for your own parish's website, just go to your browser and type in such words as: 'outstanding church websites', 'church websites', etc. There are so many good examples out there.

You may also visit various diocesan websites for both ideas and for key diocesan personnel. A good example of an archdiocesan website is included with permission from the Archdiocese of Brisbane and found at http://bne.catholic.net.au/asp/index.asp

Website Inclusions

Many good ideas can be gained from exploring the World Wide Web (WWW or Web or Internet) and noting characteristics that may be included on your website.

This exploration would be relevant both for those about to create a website and those who are / will be doing the updating.

Homepage

The homepage is the most important page to get correct. It is the page the viewer normally reaches on their initial search. First impressions are critical.

The appearance needs to be in-line with the parish's selected branding styles:

- colors
- photos (for ease of acquiring and using professional images, check out such sites as: istockphoto (http://www.istockphoto.com/index.php) and crestock.com (http://www.crestock.com/). These sites provide professional standard images at relatively inexpensive rates. You buy royalty-free images which you can then use on your website. You may, however, have good professional ones done for you. These photos need to be professionally presented. Don't skimp on costs here.)
- logo
- motto or catchphrase
- selected key words and key phrases
- good graphics
- clear, directing toolbar/s and other links
- attention grabbing inclusions e.g.
  - * news updates
  - * upcoming events
  - * webpages on your website listed

A good sample of a homepage is included with permission from The Catholic Parish of Southport and shown here and found at: http://scp.org.au/

The Toolbar needs your website's important categories displayed clearly and efficiently. Areas would usually include a number of the following:

- Home
- About Us
- Mass and (other) Sacramental Times
- Parish News
- Visitors Information
- Parish Staff
- Newsletter
- New Parishioners Information
- Emergency Contact Details
- Contact Details.

Webpage Templates

Templates for each additional webpage, following the Homepage, should be similar in appearance but allowing for the specialty of each page.

If the website has a blog, the Blog page would need specific inclusions not on any other page e.g. 'Recent Posts', 'Archive' and 'Tags'.
(More Blogging details follow shortly.)

Your exploration of good websites on the internet will help with your decisions. As styles develop, quality improves and fashions appear, your internet searches for good sites and their inclusions will be of significance to your final website templates.

Other Inclusions

These should be added as soon as possible, allowing for budget restraints, interests of the parishioners / potential parishioners and expertise of web-builders and web-managers:

- **Blogs** – these are becoming quite common amongst many parishioners, so the use of these would be considered important by many people.

    Blogs allow for interaction of website viewers with your site. Blogs are posted and people interact either by just viewing what was written or by adding their own thoughts. You have the capacity to allow all comments sent or only the selected comments you would like being viewed by your website's audience.
    (See more on Blogs later.)

    A sample introduction to a blog taken from the CPM website follows. The complete Blog Post (contents of this topic) may be found at:
    http://churchparishmarketing.com/_blog

There are also many commercially available and free to operate blogs. These will allow you to say whatever you like in varying lengths from quite substantial down to a rather restricted 140 words on Twitter.

Twitter is a rather interesting and very quickly growing mini blog.(More details on Twitter later.)

At this stage an example page is reproduced with permission from Twitter, Inc. found at http://twitter.com/

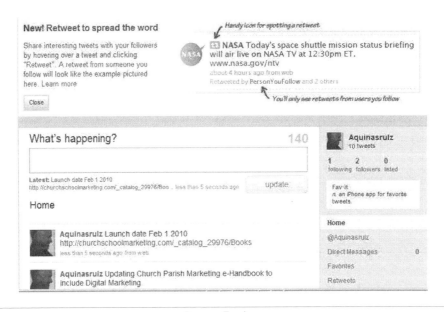

- **Photo Galleries** and **Video Galleries** are also seen by many as a necessary part of any good website. Parishes should include a selection of parish activities and involved parishioners representing a cross section of activities and parishioner demographics.

  A Photo Gallery sample is shown below and found at: http://churchparishmarketing.com/_webapp_273892/Family_Moments

- **'You Tube'** videos being embedded into your website also adds another dimension to your website. Once again, you have full control over what you add.

  Once the Parish Web Manager appreciates the management software then embedding 'You Tube' into the site's HTML is usually a simple task.

  The sample on the next page may be found embedded in the CPM website at: http://churchparishmarketing.com/

Begin or continue to develop your own marketing strategies and church, parish or deanery marketing plan with assistance from the many suggestions offered within this website.

Come back for more as this is a fluid website which continually engages the reader as it grows and develops according to the needs of those interested in an interactive website.

-us): Thanks for the great work you have been doing at Brisbane Catholic Education Centre. Your work has brought joy to my heart. ..

Rev Wally Dethlefs, Project Officer – Marginalised Students, BCE – *Archdiocese of Brisbane*

Methods - Strategies - Examples

(More on 'You Tube' later.)

- **Podcasts** - audio and video recordings highlighting key aspects of the church life, would be added to the parish website as needed. This is a different approach to embedding 'You Tube' videos or audios. Your web-builder would need to assist you with this embedding. (In addition to Podcasts see more on the Parish DVD / CD later in this e-book.)

An Archdiocesan Podcast sample has been included with permission from the Archdiocese of Brisbane and may be found at:

http://bne.catholic.net.au/asp/index.asp And click on 'Play Video' in left column.

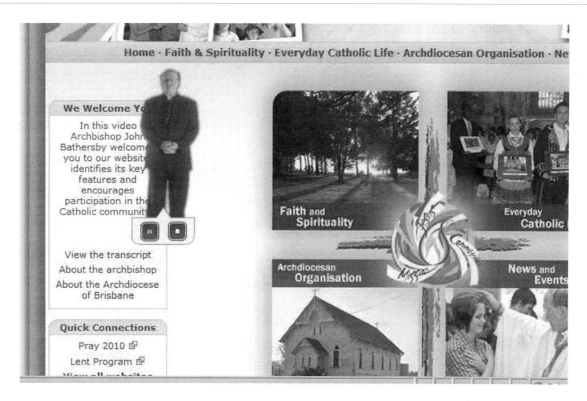

- **Social Networking** sites such as **'Facebook', 'myspace', 'LinkedIn' and 'Twitter'**, etc are also becoming the norm for many church goers. Churches will need to include these links to and from the parish website in their marketing plan.

  That is, you will need to develop a parish profile and / or parish priest profile, or other key personnel within the parish profiles, etc. at these various social networking websites and then link your website to these pages either through links or through RSS feeds.
  (More about Social Networking and RSS feeds later in this chapter.)

  You may also link from the social networking sites back to your parish website. Generally for churches, I would recommend both directional links.

Domain Names / URLs

Each website has a unique Domain Name / URL (Uniform Resource Locator). These may be purchased from a number of suppliers. Just search 'Domain Names' in your search engine and a large selection of suppliers will be found.

Most parishes would be either be linked off their diocesan website, or create their own website and hence have a unique church domain name, or have both.

You can have numerous domain names linked to your one website. This means that each time a person types any domain name linked to your website into the top URL bar of their browser the visitor would end up on your website. Most major sites only need one domain name; however others may be purchased to avoid any confusion with other institutions with similar names.

It may also be advisable to purchase similar names with key words changed to avoid confusion with other similar church names e.g. www.stmaryschurch.org and www.st-marysparish.org

Churches and Parishes would normally purchase .org or .net domains e.g.

www.stmarys.org or www.stmarys.net

However, as most people are so used to using .com it may be advisable to also include this domain as well. Hence, if visitors type your domain with a .com they would be transferred to the correct website, for example, if you had both the following:

www.stmarys.org and www.stmarys.com

Website Creation, Hosting and Costs

- **Overview**

Websites can be as simple as a few basic pages through to a highly sophisticated fully interactive commercial site.

Costs for creating the site and hosting it vary according to your selected approach. There are even free or inexpensive ways of gaining a website.

Beware of the free approaches, in case there are catches / issues of which you may not be aware. Remember that when you pay anything, or agree to their terms and conditions, you will be a part of some sort of contract – important to read the fine print.

- **Commercial website build and hosting**

If it was decided to go through a normal website creation business to build and host your website be prepared to pay anything from a few thousand to tens of thousands of dollars for the website build, depending on complexity + monthly hosting charges often between $50 and $100 (as at time of writing).

- **My Preference**

It is my preference to go through a professional website builder who also arranges for my hosting (plus I also chose the beneficial management software option). I believe this offers more peace of mind, someone to contact to meet my website adjustment / changes requirements and to answer or solve my difficulties. They also take responsibility for system breakdowns, etc. This company also has an educational component for the purchaser, which is very beneficial.

- **Caution**

There are so many offerings out there so be very careful about the decision you make – check everything out thoroughly, especially the Terms and Conditions. Don't sign anything until you are fully aware of what is offered and agree fully with this.

- **Church Website Needs**

Firstly decide what you need:

- ⋆ the purpose of your church website
- ⋆ allocated budget (this can grow in time, once confidence and availability of funds increases, etc. Best to start small than not start at all!)
- ⋆ who does the creativity overview / graphics / photos used / website design and who will build your site (saves money if someone in-house at your church does as much as possible) – quotes and appreciation of services offered are needed
- ⋆ who will oversee the whole process and keep in constant contact with web designers, which could take some time depending on the complexity
- ⋆ am I fully aware of all the implications, especially if deciding on a cheap alternative?

- **Best Website Building and Hosting Approach for Your Church?**

Decide on the best approach for your church. The two main options for most churches are:

- ⋆ Parish pays for development and website hosting and usually gets own domain name.
- ⋆ Parish links with other parishes / deanery / diocese to share development and housing costs. Each parish has its own webpages as part of a larger website. The parish name would usually be an extension of the larger group's domain name.

I mention two other options which may be worth considering. These are two growth areas for relatively inexpensive websites. I recommend you do your own research for these options and discuss with others the various implications each offers and whether either is worth pursuing for your church. Read the Terms and Conditions carefully.

- ⋆ Online web hosting and web creating services can be relatively inexpensive. Here you develop your own website following their instructions. Your site can offer the basics through to the commercial. I would tend toward the more well known companies until my experience was more complete and I appreciated the numerous options and possible pitfalls certain businesses may offer.

One example you could explore is at Yahoo http://smallbusiness.yahoo.com/

* Blogs as websites. You can develop various commercial blog sites into your own church de-facto website, sometimes for free. For a fee you can add much more than the basics offered for free. This may include your own domain / URL name, as well as designing the layout more to your style. (See Blog section in this chapter for various possible blogs worth exploring further.)

Legal Advice

You will need to also include legal statements explaining your conditions and terms of use for visitors to your website.

Statements such as on:

- **Copyright**
- **Privacy Policy**
- **Web Disclaimer**
- **Conditions of Use**
- **Blog Conditions of Use**

Most major church organizations these days would have their umbrella organization offering suggestions for these inclusions.

Otherwise, I would suggest seeking your own legal advice.

Website Management Software Sample

As an example of this sort of software, which I find enormously helpful for website administration and my 'online business / website' evaluation etc, let us explore a program called Iceberg

An informative introductory slideshow about the Iceberg software, which I have reproduced below with permission from 'Always Interactive', may be found at: http://www.alwaysinteractive.com/iceberg/quicktour/

You may also be interested in an introductory video which may be found at www.alwaysinteractive.com/iceberg/video/

Meet the first system born to run online businesses. Your website and a central customer database. Email marketing and eCommerce. Web analytics and customer profiling. It's one, central console with everything you need to run your online business.

Let's build your business online with the system built for success.

Run your website

The system will host your website and enable YOU to manage it without a programmer.

Beyond web pages, you can create a community with forums, build an audience with blogs, make secure areas for VIP content... and more.

Intro   Run Your Website   Capture Leads   Know Your Customers   An Online Shop   Send Newsletters   Executive Insight   What's Next

Capture leads

React faster - build smart web forms that notify you instantly by email and SMS when you get a new customer!

You can use a point-n-click approach to build custom web forms that capture every inquiry in a contact managment database, so you'll never lose a lead.

Intro   Run Your Website   Capture Leads   Know Your Customers   An Online Shop   Send Newsletters   Executive Insight   What's Next

Know your customers

With your online business console, every web inquiry, every purchase and every action is being recorded against a customer record.

Over time you'll get a complete picture of every customer and how they interact with your business, all from your built-in contact database.

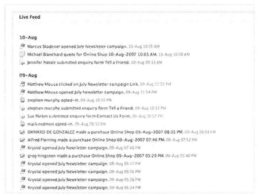

Intro   Run Your Website   Capture Leads   Know Your Customers   An Online Shop   Send Newsletters   Executive Insight   What's Next

An online shop

Set up an online shop and sell your products in a matter of minutes with your online business' online shop management features.

Without extra software, without extra effort you can sell products, fulfill orders, manage stock levels and collect payments automatically.

Next ➡

Intro Run Your Website Capture Leads Know Your Customers An Online Shop Send Newsletters Executive Insight What's Next

Send newsletters

Email marketing is the most effective form of marketing available to a business owner.

With your online business console, you can send newsletters and other campaigns to targeted lists of customers that you've saved in Online Business Console' built-in contact database.

Next ➡

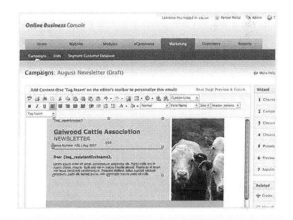

Intro Run Your Website Capture Leads Know Your Customers An Online Shop Send Newsletters Executive Insight What's Next

Executive insight

Log in, and you're greeted with an instant overview of how your business is tracking from 4 key metrics.

From there you can drill down into detailed reports on your website, marketing campaigns and e-commerce performance.

Next ➡

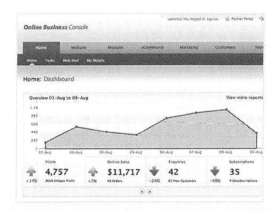

Intro Run Your Website Capture Leads Know Your Customers An Online Shop Send Newsletters Executive Insight What's Next

Once you begin using software such as this, you should have available to you from the supplier considerable 'help desk' assistance. This Iceberg program does. If other management software you are considering does not, I would suggest seriously considering your options.

RSS Feeds

RSS (Really Simple Syndication) feeds allow for your website visitors to register to receive updates you make to selected webpages which have this additional RSS capacity.

Advantages of RSS

Active websites are continually updating the information available to visitors to their sites. To make it as simple as possible for interested visitors to receive your updated information, you could make various webpages on your website RSS feed active i.e. if people register for receiving your updates they will receive these as your updates become available.

For churches the most likely RSS activation would be for their:

- e-newsletter
- sacramental / ceremony times and dates
- blog pages.

In time you would become aware of which pages you continually update and hence would be of interest to parishioners and other interested people. These could then be added to the RSS list.

Simple methods are shown below for:

- creating RSS feeds on your website and
- receiving selected RSS feeds.

Symbols

is the common RSS feed symbol appearing on most websites and found at http://www.microsoft.com/technet/security/bulletin/secrssinfo.mspx .

Sample Website with RSS facility

For a sample website look at http://churchparishmarketing.com/ . On this website pages offering this facility are:

- Blogs
- News
- Hints and Tips
- Specials

However, you may link virtually as many of your website's webpages through RSS Feeds as you desire, as long as your website's management system has the capacity.

Church Website Developers adding RSS Feeds

Good website management software has the capacity to add RSS links for your webpages. This should be a simple procedure.

An example is from the CPM website. Here we use the Iceberg management software from Always Interactive as shown below and available at http://www.alwaysinteractive.com/

Only four fields need to be completed before pressing 'Save':

- RSS Channel Name
- Update Frequency
- RSS Channel Description
- Enable (for page to go live)

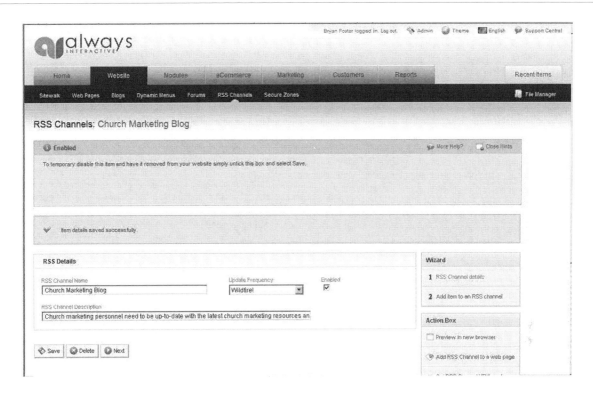

There are many websites which have various offers for adding RSS feeds to your website. A quick search of your search engines will show the many options worth exploring. Use terms such as 'adding RSS feed to website' for best results.

Once again, I very much favor the software management option.

Visitors Subscribing to a RSS Feed

1. Click the RSS feeds symbol, e.g. 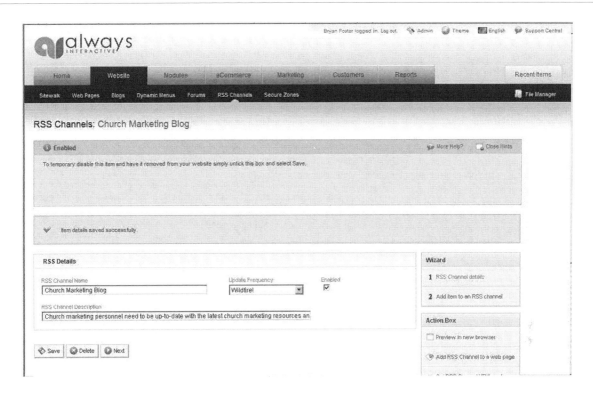, on the page where the symbol occurs: either on the webpage itself or on the browser toolbar with that page
2. Click 'Subscribe to this Feed'
3. Give the feed a title
4. Select the folder for the feed
5. Click 'Subscribe'

RSS Symbol Location for a Webpage

The RSS symbol will usually appear in color when active either on the:

- browser's toolbar of the page offering RSS feeds or
- webpage itself which is offering the RSS feed.

Sample RSS Feed

An example of an RSS feed from the CPM website follows.

Click on the  orange RSS feed symbol on the toolbar of the browser at http://churchparishmarketing.com/_blog in this following screen.

This webpage below then appears.

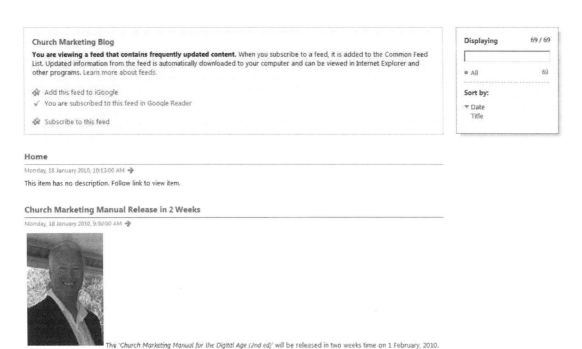

Follow the prompts as you make your selections from the screen above.

When you click on 'Subscribe to this feed' on your browser on the above screen, you will go to http://churchparishmarketing.com/RSSRetrieve.aspx?ID=2480&Type=RSS20 , which is shown below.

This now becomes a part of the 'Favorites' section in your browser.

RSS Symbol Different Location

If we looked at the 'News' page on the CPM website, we would find the RSS symbol on the webpage itself – just above the beginning of the News' article. We would click on this to subscribe and make the appropriate selections. (See http://churchparishmarketing.com/news)

Viewing RSS Feeds

- 'Favorites' - To view these RSS feeds created in your 'Favorites', all you need to do is click on the 'Favorites' button on your browser toolbar, select 'Feeds' tab and there are the Feeds.

- 'iGoogle' or 'Google Reader' - Another popular option for the placement of the feeds is at Google - going to 'iGoogle' or 'Google Reader'. All you need to do is select either of these options in that first selection box above. You will need to register for these options separately though.

- Other options also exist. See Microsoft link below as an example.

RSS Feeds Further Explained

You will also notice in two screens above that when you click on the 'Learn more about feeds' blue link the right hand column called 'Using feeds (RSS)' appears. Follow this column down for a good explanation of the FAQs (Frequently Asked Questions) about RSS feeds.

Another professional presentation, including other options, is done by Microsoft and may be found at http://www.microsoft.com/technet/security/bulletin/secrssinfo.mspx

Further explanations of RSS are also available from various websites – just search through your browsers.

Search Engine Optimization (SEO) for Church Websites

To gain higher positioning at various search engines such as Google, Yahoo, You Tube, Bing, Baidu (China) and AOL Search, etc various methods of SEO are needed.

Website Viewers

Some churches and parishes aren't really interested in having their website visited from people all over the world. These worshipping communities are more interested in their local congregations. For these people SEOs are not needed.

Various communities might like their website to be easily accessible to people from various parts of their particular country but not necessarily beyond their borders. This allows for people transferring to their parish to preview what their parish has to offer. A suggestion for these communities would be to select a domain name which ends in their countries code e.g. United Kingdom .uk, for Australia .au, etc.

Other communities may be interested in having their church and their website open worldwide. SEOs would likely suit these churches.

Suggestions for Improvement

Some ways I have found which I believe help with Search Engine Optimization are:

- The **Domain name** includes the church / parish name and suburb.

- **Key Words** such as the church / parish name are regularly used throughout the site, particularly in titles / headings, first sentence and last sentence on each webpage.

- Each webpage within the website would highlight something different about the parish and hence also include **other key words** associated both with the parish name / suburb and that webpage's emphasis.

These other Key Words may be: sacrament, parishioner, visitor, Baptism, Marriage, mass times, contact, parish priest, priests, parish kit, open day, school or welfare groups within the parish, etc.

- Each **Blog**'s title, first and last sentences would include key words associated with that individual blog's message and that it eventuated from your parish.

- The more **links coming to your website** from other sources, particularly **.gov, .edu and .org** the better. Having other sites point to your website helps SEO i.e. having other sites have your Domain / URL linked live on their website.

  However, it is best not to swap links with others of similar level e.g. .org. That is, if each site has the other's site linked from their site, this usually causes it to neutralize the impact for both sites.

  Yet swapping these links may **improve traffic to your site**, just not higher SEO.

- Include **links within your own site** to various other webpages on your site.

- Another way of achieving the links from other sites may be achieved by developing various **Blogs elsewhere** which include the link to your website. (More on this in Blogs later.)

- **Be careful not to overdo all these links and key words as search engines may penalize you for being overambitious in gaining notice for your website.**

- **Age of the website.** Older sites have more credibility. Develop your website as soon as possible.

- **Update your site** regularly. A fresh, updated site is appealing to both visitors and for SEO.

Blogs

This is becoming a very popular form of interactive, digital communication by internet users. Content may be brief or extensive. 'Blog' is the commonly used abbreviation for 'Weblog'.

Blogs

Blogs are used to allow interaction between the website's administrator/s and the website's visitors.

Churches could benefit considerably through the effective use of Blogs. These are ideal avenues to promote your church / parish and the various messages you wish to place in the public or private domain.

These days so many people wish to be valued through their involvement and feedback - blogs are one highly regarded avenue for them to achieve this.

Blog Posts

The website's / blog's administrators write a Blog Post (comment, information, news, challenge etc.) and publish this to their website's blog page. Blog Posts may also include photos, videos, audios and other graphic presentations.

The visitor to your website's blog page would then have the option to comment on your blog post's content.

Blog Posts may be of any length and literary style depending on the target audience. However, in most cases, brevity is the norm in these days of mass communication overload. Think newspaper article lengths for most blog posts. As a general guide I work on 200-300 words per blog post.

You need to make sure that the administrator has the option to accept or reject all comments posted in response to the blog post. If the blog post is available to the public, you need to be prepared to receive all sorts of comments, including spam (mainly advertising links). Unsuitable comments would then be deleted.

Two Major Blog Uses for Churches

Church Marketers could use blogs in two primary ways:

- Parish website Blog
- External Blog sites, which you would point (link) back to your parish website.

Church Website's Blog

The church website would include a Blog page. On this page there would be the blog posts listed in sequential order with the most recent placed at the top of the page.

The Blog Page would also normally include: 'Recent Posts', an 'Archive' of previous blog posts and previous 'Tags' (key words used to attract attention to each specific blog post).

It is important to also include 'Blog Condition of Use' details on your website. An example of one may be found at: http://churchparishmarketing.com/blog

Legal advice should be sort to ascertain your particular needs.

A Sample Blog Page is at:
http://churchparishmarketing.com/_blog

Management Software

To administer the Blog page, as for all the other webpages, etc on the parish website, you will need either a good appreciation of website building software or access to reasonably simple management software to achieve the task. I use Iceberg (Business Catalyst) through Always Interactive at: http://alwaysinteractive.com/

The example below shows one such blog post's administration page. This is where you complete the details for each blog post, including the:

- Title
- Release Date
- Tags
- Blog Content.

You can insert:

- photos
- videos
- tables
- various web links etc.

There are also a large variety of other options for the presentation e.g. color, fonts, letter size, wrap-around etc.

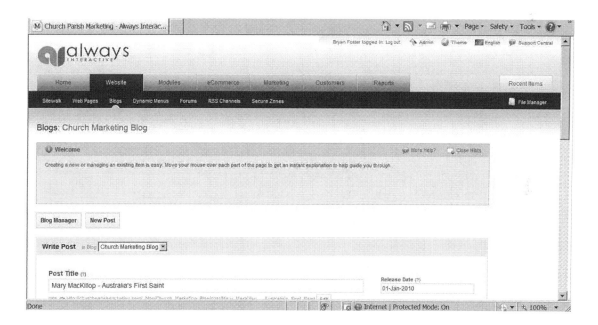

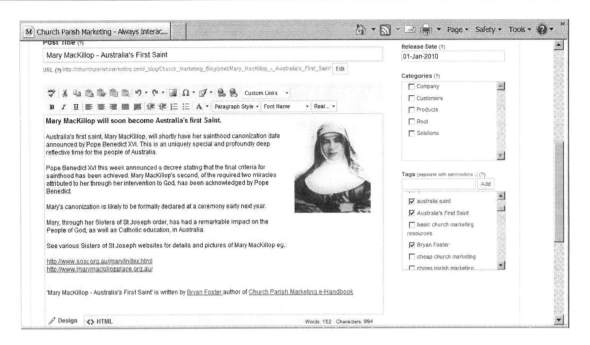

External Blog Sites

The external blog site could be used for three main reasons:

- these increase traffic to your parish website through the links you include in the general blog template you create, and also in the blog posts you write, which are directed to your parish's website
- these assist with your website's SEO (Search Engine Optimization) as each point (link) back to your parish website assists the SEO
- in most cases these external blogs are free of charge.(Costs are optional depending on your usage and on the Blog provider. In most cases you can easily do this free of charge.)

A good example of these external blogs is provided by **Blogger**.

Following is an example of both the Blogs and Blogs Posts for Blogger. There is also information to start the development of Blogger and WordPress blogs.

Also included are domain listings for other popular external blog sites.

Blogger

Blogger Homepage may be found at: http://www.blogger.com/start

An example of a Blogger Blog Post may be found at: http://meaning-of-life-is-love.blogspot.com/

To create a Blogger Account you first of all need to create a Google Account as Blogger belongs to Google. You then follow the 'Continue' key to create the Blogger Account.

To create a Blogger Account go to: https://www.blogger.com/start . Initially click on 'Create a Blog'.

(Images of the web pages you need to complete online follow.)

The page below will then appear at: https://www.google.com/accounts/ NewAccount?service=blogger&continue=https%3A%2F%2Fwww.blogger. com%2Floginz%3Fd%3D%252Fcreate-blog

Click on 'Continue' to go to next page for 'Name your blog': http://www.blogger.com/ create-blog.g?pli=1

The new Blogger account and new blog naming process is now complete.

All you need to do now is select the template (how your blog will appear)

http://www.blogger.com/choose-template

and then start putting in as much, or as little, detail you so desire about your church and / or self and then begin blogging... Enjoy!

Other External Blogs

- **WordPress**

  The WordPress Homepage can be found at: http://wordpress.com/

  An example of a WordPress blog is found at: http://meaningoflifeislove. wordpress.com/2010/01/12/love-and-forgiveness/
  To create a WordPress Account go to: http://en.wordpress.com/signup/

- **Squarespace**

  This is relatively new to the blogging scene with numerous outstanding features. Costs from $US8 to $US50 per month at time of writing. Worth a look. Very impressive reviews from the Wall Street Journal Online and CNET Webware. http://www.squarespace.com/

- **TypePad**

  TypePad was launched in 2003 and has been used by major corporations such as BBC – quite a broad spread of users. Found at: http://www.typepad.com/pro/#2 Costs from $US8.95 to $US89.95 per month at time of writing.

- Other common blogs are available at:

  http://www.joomla.org/
  http://www.movabletype.org/
  http://www.tumblr.com/
  http://www.vox.com/

Conclusion

The Blogger World is an exciting and often time consuming pastime or profession…

There are so many uses both from the church marketing perspective as well as a personal perspective. Personally I have developed the two Blogs on my official websites at:
Church Marketing Blog site
School Marketing Blog site

as well as a number of Blogs, some of these you will see linked in this e-book:
Blogger
WordPress
LinkedIn (some of these you would have seen linked in this chapter).

Once you begin on the Blogging path you will find so many uses, particularly in being able to espouse your viewpoints to the world! And have people throughout the world respond!

Email

Stakeholders within the parish, especially staff and parishioners, need to be encouraged to communicate by email.

When used correctly, email is an efficient, quick form of written communication.

Considerable communication with commercial, pastoral and educational interests associated with the parish will occur through email discussions / correspondence.

Protocols

Protocols of email usage should be followed.

Even though there appears to be growth occurring in these protocols, it would be fair to say that an email is virtually an electronic note or letter and should be treated as such.

It is not a text / txt message similar to use with a mobile / cell phone or a 'Twitter' comment (see 'Twitter' input later).

Correct language, grammar and punctuation are needed.

When it is sent at a professional level e.g. staff to staff, staff to parishioners and vice versa, professional writing protocols should be observed.

Staff Email

Staff emails need to be permanently configured so as to be based on a uniform template format which includes: Name, Title, Parish Address, Phone Number, Fax Number, Mobile / Cell Number and Skype Number, if appropriate, Email address and Web Address.

Other additions, such as a background, photo and qualifications may also be added.

Email Disclaimer

Also needed is a relevant disclaimer statement that follows all other detail.

An example is noted below:

"Unless stated otherwise, this email, together with any attachments, is intended for the named recipient(s) only and may contain privileged and confidential information. If received in error, you are asked to inform the sender as quickly as possible and delete this email and any copies of this from your computer system network.

If not an intended recipient of this email, you must not copy, distribute or take any action(s) that relies on it; any form of disclosure, modification, distribution and/or publication of this email is also prohibited.

Unless stated otherwise, this email represents only the views of the sender and not the views of [Parish Name and Suburb etc]."

Staff should try and respond within the day to any emails, however this is not always possible and hence parishioners need to be aware of the busyness of parish life and of parish staff restrictions, and to make allowances for any delay.

Legal Advice

Legal or diocesan advice for any legal or similar type of statement on your email is recommended.

Email Challenges

When staff are responding to difficulties it is often best to approach these as challenges and to be treated with respect with the aim of getting a solution.

Emails should not take the place of interviews and telephone conversations when these others are the more appropriate form of communication.

Emails should not be used to hide behind!

Parishioners who believe they have gained a satisfactory result after such email/s and telephone call/s or interview/s often become the best marketing advocates for the parish.

As they often say, "The parish listens to me!"

Email Providers

There are a number of formats and providers for emails:

- You may choose to use software such as Windows Outlook operating on your computer and linking though your normal internet provider.

- You may choose this facility to be added to your own website in the form of a 'Contact Us' form, etc.

- A common format is the webmail available through various internet websites e.g. Google's Gmail and Yahoo's email, along with your internet provider's email.

Gmail welcome page may be found by clicking <u>Gmail</u>. It will appear as below.

<u>(https://www.google.com/accounts/ServiceLogin?service=mail&passive=true&rm=false &continue=https%3A%2F%2Fmail.google.com%2Fmail%2F%3Fui%3Dhtml%26zy%3Dl&bsv =zpwhtygjntrz&ss=1&scc=1&ltmpl=default&ltmplcache=2&hl=en)</u>

Yahoo Help (Sign-in and Registration) page is found at:

http://help.yahoo.com/l/us/yahoo/edit/

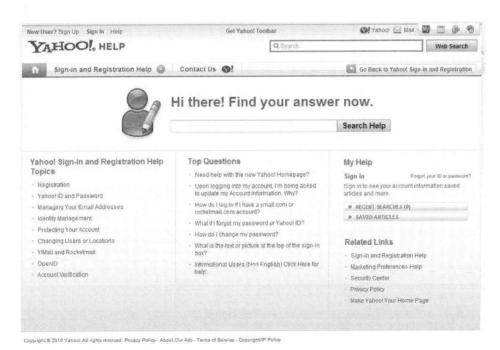

(Reproduced with permission of Yahoo! Inc. ©2010 Yahoo! Inc. YAHOO! and the YAHOO! logo are registered trademarks of Yahoo! Inc.)

e/i-Newsletter

The Parish Newsletter is often the best regular form of information-giving to parishioners. Either the e-newsletter (sent out via email) or the i-newsletter (placed on the church internet website) or both, are popular in this digital age.

e-Newsletter / i-Newsletter + Newsletter Essential

Both e-newsletter or i-newsletter will add to the target audience. Not only would it appeal to the internet / email savvy, it also becomes available to the non-weekly church attendee, the ill and for those away from the parish for varying lengths of time for innumerable reasons. That is, it is available for anyone requesting an email out from the church or to have the option of reading it on the parish website.

Supplement these with the regular hardcopy available from the church for those in attendance or on a mail-out list and interested, or not interested in an e/i-newsletter, and the target base should be considerably more.

This section within this chapter will concentrate on the e-Newsletter / i-Newsletter. The hardcopy Newsletter will also be covered in the 'Church Marketing: Necessities' chapter.

Regular Weekly Publication

Regular weekly publication is needed for best success. Regularity rules!

The readership should often be expanded to church schools and other interested parishes and even to other willing sources e.g. parent and school businesses for display in reception rooms, offices, etc.

The parish's website needs to be updated weekly with each e-newsletter uploaded to it. A collection of the year's i-newsletters on the website is appreciated by many parishioners and others wanting to get an overview of the year's progress.

The e-newsletter would be either emailed to all interested parishioners and others as per a developed database and / or placed on the website as an i-newsletter. I would suggest both as people are more likely to read the email sent to them. Having the website archive as a backup helps considerably for people checking for previous e/i-newsletters / news, etc.

Professional e-Newsletter / i-Newsletter

A professional publication is needed.

The parish's branding is very important and needs to be strategically positioned on the pages / website.

Photos 'tell a thousand words' and whenever possible should be used. Appropriate content, quality and sizing are essential for success.

This is especially true for an e/i-Newsletter where bright, interesting photos seem to 'often come to life' and add significantly to the effectiveness of the presentation. Hence the impact on the way in which each story is received by the reader.

The presentation can be quite outstanding when displayed on LCD monitors – use colors, text, images and layout wisely for maximum impact.

(However, paper copies should also be produced for presentation at the front of the churches and in the Parish and School Offices.)

e-Newsletter / i-Newsletter Homepage +

Begin with the Homepage, usually written by the Parish Priest. Parishioners tend to read the points from the leader of the church / parish first, and possibly only these. This homepage should include at least all the summarized main points from the e/i-newsletter.

The next page, or as the reader scrolls down, links to all the other articles.

When the link is clicked each of the articles appears on its own.

Production: In-house or Outsourced

The e/i-Newsletter may be produced through the parish as either an emailed publication i.e. an attachment, or as an attached webpage to the church's and school's websites.

The e-Newsletter may be outsourced to professional e/i-Newsletter producers. The firms usually don't charge much, however they require you to allow advertising by them on the e/i-Newsletter.

An example business is 'Always Interactive' which has a worldwide service available for churches and schools. The promotional material is primarily still targeted towards their successful schools' program (in the process of changing) yet show exactly what can be done for churches. To view the options go to their present website at http://www.school-zine.com.au/

"The majority of the production cost is subsidized by national companies and local businesses that pay 'Schoolzine' to advertise tastefully in the E-Newsletters. This allows [churches] to pay only a fraction of the cost. Only family friendly advertising is published in the e-newsletters and all with final approval from the [church]." (Schoolzine promotional literature)

Effectiveness

It can be argued that most people read only the front page, which is usually written by the Parish Priest. If this is the case then the most important detail needs to be included here.

It follows that the newsletter's length be appropriate so that time and money is not wasted.

A good coverage of recent and upcoming events and activities, including service times, is the primary purpose of the newsletter.

Some form of weekly rotation of topics / staff or parishioners presenting articles may be needed for effectiveness. This would especially apply if there are many writers and topics to be covered.

Staff and parishioner leaders should be encouraged to participate but according to certain parameters, especially length.

Brevity Rulz

Brevity is once again paramount to these stories.

This is often difficult for many people. These people need to be educated as to the best means of getting their information read in the newsletter.

Most importantly, staff and parishioner leaders need to feel valued for their input to the newsletter.

Advertising Dilemma

Many believe that the church should not be seen as a commercial enterprise but as a stand-alone religious institute.

They may also argue that advertisements aren't usually read, yet the placement can vary considerably due to the nature of webpages.

Electronic advertising is often more intrusive due to the high quality of the presentation and the special use of colors and design used to attract attention.

Advertisements need to be carefully selected so as to not impose on the overall production. The main purpose of the newsletter is not to advertise certain products.

When outsourced, churches need to be in philosophical alignment with the outsourced company's principles of advertising and the particular adverts used.

If the church can negotiate their own suppliers as advertisers, this should result in better success for the parish, due to the often localized nature of the adverts i.e. supporting the local community and all the goodwill this generates.

The decision often comes down to the church's budgetary restraints.

Layout Development

Churches may have one or two staff that receive and do the newsletter's layout. This is good organizational practice.

If staff and parishioner leaders can electronically send their stories this improves the time taken and in a number of ways the effectiveness of the presentation. Electronic methods would be through the parish's computer networks or as an email attachment.

This method should be considered essential for economy of time and expense reasons.

The attachments should include photos (+ captions explaining the photo, including the names of people from left to right) and directions to where photos are stored if on any server.

The Parish Priest, or designated staff member, would need to decide on specific articles for each week's publication. Some articles may need to be delayed in line with the rotation method of weekly article selection.

> **Proofing is essential!**

e/ i-Flyer

e-Flyers / i-Flyers are issued electronically whenever some important news or event is forthcoming. When these appear on the church internet website the term i-Flyer is more accurate. Brevity and presentation is the secret.

Theme

A specific theme for each flyer needs to be apparent e.g. Holy Week, Advent / Christmas, Social Justice Programs, Youth Events or Aged Care Developments, etc.

Other themes may be linked from the e/i-flyer, but best not to distract from the main theme. Most of the content and images visible should be based on the main theme.

Be aware that having a general themed flyer to promote the church will often say to the reader that the parish needs more people. Many people react against this.

Frequency

Due to the ease of production and success that these flyers invariably bring, it is important not to overdo the frequency of email-outs and / or website postings. It would be hard to imagine the need for a frequency of less than fortnightly – so that the readers do not develop a blasé approach to the e/i-Flyers.

Purpose

The purpose is to inform the parishioners, potential families and other interested parties of the advantages of your church to the community through its ongoing prayer-life, communal activities and developments.

This should create a positive discussion. The prestige of the parish should be raised or confirmed. Interest should be increased with potential new families to your church and parish.

Distribution Methods

There are two main ways to distribute the flyers:

- e-Flyers are emailed: from parish or third party production
- i-Flyer on the church internet website.

Email-outs

The e-flyer is either sent out directly via email attachment from the parish or is sent via a third party who publishes the e-flyer for you.

It is best to then to also place the e-flyer on your church website.

Its placement on the website would depend on how you have decided to name your webpages e.g. it would be best to have its own webpage 'i-Flyers', however the i-flyers could also be included on your 'News' or 'e/i-Newsletter' pages etc.

Production of e-Flyers

A good e-flyer can be put together using the basic software - 'Office Word' or 'Office Publisher'. Otherwise, you may like to use more professional publishing programs, but these are usually not necessary, unless you have the expertise needed.

Often it is best to get a professional, usually your website's designer, to create **e/i-flyer and e/i-newsletter templates** based on your church website's templates. You then add the information and images (sometimes with graphics) as needed.

Database for email-outs

Create a database of the interested parishioners and other individuals and groups, particularly including the email addresses.

i-Flyer Webpage

The simplest and easiest, yet least effective, method to publish an i-flyer, is to place it only on your website.

If using this method, it would be a good idea to have a special webpage named 'i-flyer', or something similar which draws attention to its urgent / high priority nature.It should be placed on the specially created i-flyer template webpage.The adding of content to this page would be of a similar nature to adding content to any of the other webpages on your website. Knowledge of these skills is necessary.

Layout

The heading / title would be devoted to the theme e.g. Holy Week.

Follow this with key points and necessary detail. Remember the golden rule of marketing – **brevity, clarity and presentation.**

Place **attractive photos**, based on your theme, to gain greatest appeal. Captions often essential.

Photos, brief text, color and branding (though the well developed template) are key aspects of any flyer.

Size of e-Flyer / i-Flyer

Often the best sized flyer is the equivalent of an A4 page.

You may also include links from the e-flyer / i-flyer to other webpages you would like linked, including your 'i-Newsletter', 'News' and 'Service Times' webpages.

Try not to allow these links to distract from your flyer's theme but to compliment it. Often the best position for links is at the bottom of the page. However, there would be times when linking directly from the text or image would be necessary or suitable.

A high quality production is necessary.

Production – Offsite Option

You may like to do everything onsite or send all resources to your third party e-flyer / i-flyer producer.

Production is similar to creating an advertisement:

- Sketch layout according to decided theme and placement on a e/i-flyer template

- Arrange images' placement. (Each image needs to be large enough to clearly see the required detail. Captions are often necessary to compliment the photo's message.)

- Write the text (e.g. Easter Sunday Service text would need the details of the day including times, venue, roles, post community activities, etc.)

- Select photos from any rehearsals, Good Friday services or last year's service, etc.

- Arrange for the taking of any other pics (photos) you need

- Make final photo selections (each photo tells a thousand words.)

- Discuss layout, texts and pics with the Parish Priest or designated personnel

- Include contact details for the parish, especially addresses, website address, email address and phone number, at bottom of main page

- Proof all text and images

- Send sketches, images and texts for the e/i-flyer to the producers for layout arranging (unless completed at the Parish Office or through a parishioner's generosity – then send digital file by email or CD)

- Proof drafts received back, usually by email from producers, with the Parish Priest or other key personnel. Send back to producers for updating.

- Read final draft and when all changes have been made sign-off for publishing.

- Producers will now email this out to all on the database you have provided.

- Upload i-flyer to website.

Social Networking Website Use for Churches

Churches can benefit from appropriate, and sometimes creative, use of social networking sites. Increasingly, this form of communication is becoming more obvious for parishes. Be aware of all the privacy and legal issues!

The Challenge

Once again we are challenged to meet our parishioners where they are at, or might be, in the near future.

The **social networking tentacles are reaching further into the various demographics affecting our parish communities,** often way beyond the awareness of church leaders.

No longer is it just the **teens and '20 something'**, it is **now common for people in their 50s and 60s** to have one or more social networking accounts.

The Misconception

With respect, and only to make a point shout out loudly, the misconception is that this form of communication is just used for inane chat amongst 'dizzy lightweights'!

Yes, this may be so for a number of users, however there is a considerably large and ever growing group of people who use this for much more than chat, even though legitimate chat does play an important part in many forms of communication.

These people are not only building and strengthening relationships amongst friends and newly formed acquaintances / friends through their engagement online with each other and often doing so simultaneously, they may also be **adding depth to key aspects of their lives**.

Assumptions Underlying Social Networking Websites?

There are a number of interesting assumptions an ever expanding group of people, with representatives in most age groups, of the 21st century make:

- People like to build trusting relationships with others before doing 'business' (Churches need to be open to appreciating this belief and then adapting the way they communicate with such people.)
- The busyness of life often limits face-to-face opportunities
- The relationship does not need to be a face-to-face encounter, even though this is often preferred
- 'anonymity' allows for a less inhibited sharing of ideas and thoughts. (Easier for some people to make a comment when the contact person isn't actually in front of them. Similar for some people when using telephones or email.)
- The internet often provides the answers people are seeking (How often do you hear more and more, "Google it!")
- Digital communication is the easiest and quickest means of communication
- Digital communication allows for multiple conversations simultaneously
- People using these forms of communication eventually trust in the results due to their experiences.

Why Consider Social Networking Websites?

> **To reach this ever growing group of people in our communities we must meet them where they are at!**

In many circumstances, this may not be your 'cup of tea'. But you do have control over who sees and comments on your church 'Facebook' pages if you follow the security directions. You may limit membership to only parishioners and hence only these people will see what you say and show.

> **It is, however, a successful method of informing an ever growing group of your community of whatever it is you would like to inform them about.**

The example below of the St Mary's Parish, Coomera, shows some ways social network-ing sites e.g. Facebook is used by church parishes:

- Parish and Contact Details
- News from the Parish Priest and Responses from Parishioners
- News about Youth and Children's Activities and Responses
- Upcoming Parish Events
- Parish Photos
- Parish Priest Recommended Websites for Parishioners

Which Sites to Use

There are literally over 150 social networking sites available. An interesting article that explains the numerous options can be found at http://en.wikipedia.org/wiki/List_of_social_networking_websites

It is generally agreed that the top three most popular sites, and hence the ones used by most parishioners, are 'Facebook', 'myspace' and 'Twitter'. 'LinkedIn' is at #5 and growing quickly.

This *Church Marketing Manual for the Digital Age (2nd ed)* will concentrate on samples and instructions from: Facebook, Twitter and LinkedIn. Each website has its detail explained separately. Mention will be made of myspace.

Approaches to Use

There are two main approaches to using these social networking sites:

- As a church group
- As an church leader within the parish

Church Group Membership

Social networking sites have the capacity for you to form a religious group for your church.

I do not claim to be an expert in all the ways of any social networking site. I suggest that if you explore the social networking sites in greater depth plus various discussion boards, chat rooms, blogs and use your search engines and the websites these find on the internet you will gain a fuller appreciation of the positives and negatives of these sites.

For me these steps have been successful and up until this stage I have been more than happy with the results.

Church Leader Membership

The church leader often gains considerable esteem from the parishioners who are social networking members or who may be considering being members.

The leader would often be the Parish Priest, Pastoral Associate or Parish Manager or other parish leader as decided by the parish leadership team. Of course anyone may have membership, **yet to speak on behalf of the parish the person would need leadership approval**.

This page could be used for basic communication similar to a newsletter, or for whatever the parish priest or leadership team decides. It could be creatively used by these people to:

- Develop higher profiles
- Show another side to their personality, interests, etc.
- Explain their thoughts, beliefs and feelings on particular issues

Or to promote various happenings, such as:

- particular events or activities in which they participate

Or to:

- Encourage involvement of others within the parish community.

Caution - As with any use of the internet, privacy will always be an issue. The more information placed on the internet the more potential for this information being misused.

I would suggest that special care is taken with what is added to the internet.

I personally and professionally support the use of the internet. I believe that it has opened up so many positive options both personally and professionally.

I am always aware that I need to take due care with what I add to the internet. If in doubt, always seek legal advice.

Check each social networking's privacy, safety and legal advice.

Facebook

Individual Sign Up Page

If you would like to set up an individual / personal Facebook page, go to the link below and follow the instructions similar to for the Group setup.

To create a **Facebook** account go to: http://www.facebook.com/

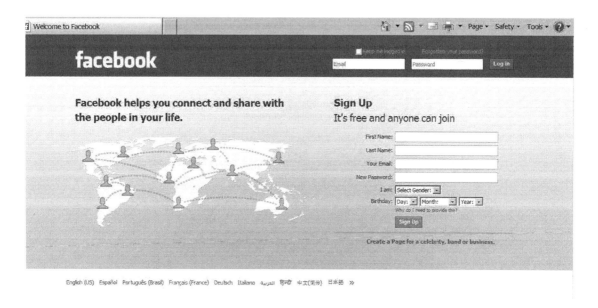

Sample Parish Priest Account

A sample Facebook page extract by a Parish Priest is shown below with permission granted from Fr Adrian Sharp PP at http://www.facebook.com/adrian.sharp2?ref=ts

Religious Organization Sample

The following information and screen is included to help you with your development of a religious group 'Facebook' page. These steps have worked for me on a number of occasions.

A parish which I have been heavily involved with for over a decade now has its own 'Facebook' group page. The St Mary's Catholic Community, Coomera 'Info' page is shown below with permission granted from Fr Adrian Sharp PP at:

http://www.facebook.com/group.php?gid=14891935948&ref=search&sid=1418024383.3181693141..1

The St Mary's Coomera 'Wall' page where members can add their own comments is shown below with permission granted from Fr Adrian Sharp PP at:

http://www.facebook.com/group.php?v=wall&ref=search&gid=14891935948

Messages are commonly added to the site e.g. the one below is found at: http://www.facebook.com/reqs.php

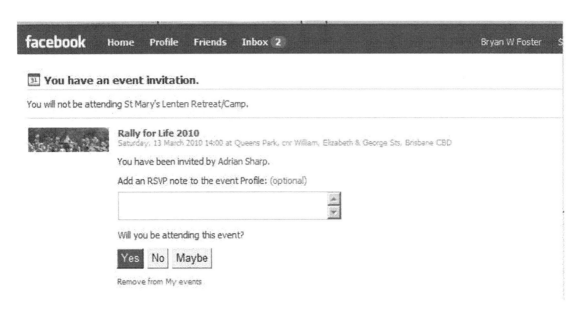

There are also various other religious organizations apart from churches and parishes using Facebook. To find out what organizations have Facebook pages, just do a search when on a Facebook page. You will need to be a member of Facebook to do this.

One such example is the Australian Confraternity of Catholic Clergy (ACCC) in Queensland found on Facebook at:

http://www.facebook.com/group.php?gid=146341449337

Religious Organization Sign Up Steps Sample

As an example to show how to set up a Facebook group page, follow the webpages:

You begin on this Facebook homepage for membership @ http://www.facebook.com/

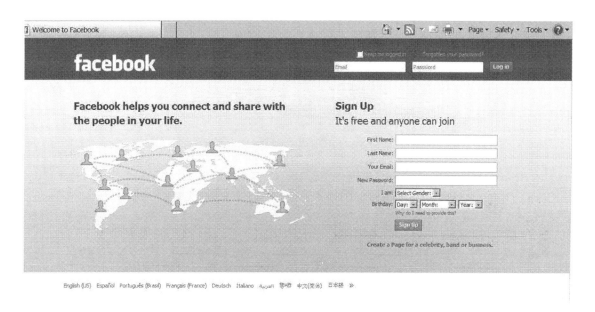

Next click on the bottom of this page where it says: "Create a Page for a celebrity, band or business. You then end up at the screen below.

Here select 'Brand, Product, or Organization' then scroll down and select 'Religious Organization'.

Next place the name of your Facebook page in the 'Name of Page' box. This would normally be the church / parish name and suburb. (The suburb helps differentiate from all the other churches in the world with your church's name.)

Tick the box just below so that this page won't go live on the internet just yet. I wanted to add to my profile.

Complete the security check further down by placing the unclear letters from the box into the 'Text in the box' box.

Link Religious Organization to Twitter?

When you go to the next page it will ask if you wish to link your new group page to your Twitter account. (See more about Twitter shortly.)

(For my newly formed group the next page appeared at: http://www.facebook.com/pages/Love-is-the-Meaning-of-Life/265813695571?created)

(Twitter Homepage may be found at: http://twitter.com/)

If you have a Twitter account this would probably be a good idea if you wanted to let your Twitter 'friends' see what you have added to your church Facebook site.

If you don't have a Twitter account (you can always make one later and come back to complete this request), or you do not want information you add to this site to go to Twitter, and then don't click on that option.

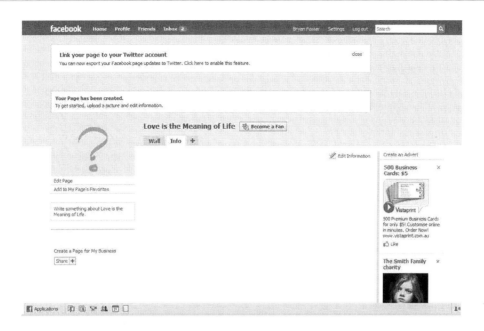

If you do click positively on this option you will end up looking at a similar page to this link:

https://twitter.com/oauth/authorize?oauth_token=w7vv0SUaJzN5xAseicYUCXphnvZ9xpf
KJIA5ePeyrXo

I now have an account. At this stage I click on the name of my account i.e. 'Meaning of Life is Love' on the screen above (when it is live on my computer). The following screen comes up for me at: http://www.facebook.com/pages/Love-is-the-Meaning-of-Life/265813695571

This is where we now add our initial detail about the parish by clicking on 'Edit Information' on the right side.

We then add the various security levels, such as who can access the information, etc by clicking on 'Edit Page' in left column.Then follow the prompts and complete as needed. There are many sections where you do not have to add anything if you do not want to… Just add what you are comfortable with.

Facebook FAQs and Help Webpages

A good selection of Frequently Asked Questions and Help for Facebook can be found at:

http://www.facebook.com/help/

Caution

I suggest that you read the following before commencing a 'Facebook' account to make sure this is best for you and your church.

Explore the Facebook Help webpage at http://www.facebook.com/help/ for Privacy, Security, Warnings, Intellectual Property, and Accessibility can be found at:

Twitter

Twitter is basically an abbreviated Blog. It allows members instant messaging of thoughts of no more than 140 characters / spaces. Tweets (responses) may also be added by mobile phone.

Church Uses

- **Instant Feedback**

One key use of 'Twitter' could be to gain **instant appreciation of parishioners' thoughts** on a topic. A data-projector could display the parish's Twitter page on a large screen and parishioners could instantly add their thoughts via their mobile phone to the account which would then be seen on the large screen instantly. This would give both instant feedback plus a record of views.

An example could be: a parishioner offers a social activity proposal and parishioners are invited to offer their first thoughts. Subsequent thoughts could be relayed later on. These are then taken to the social committee for a decision and arrangement of the event.

The church website may include a link to the parish's Twitter account.

- **Interactive Homily**

The **modern priest** could also include this as part of an **interactive homily**.

However, this could be open to problems, such as inappropriate 'live' comments. I do believe that in time this interactive homily will actually occur in various parishes and suitable situations.

Various protocols and parameters will be developed to suit individual parishes, etc.

- **Keeping in Contact**

This is another contemporary method for parishioners to keep in contact with key parish personnel and vice versa.

It allows for **brevity of thought** – an often growing method of communication today. There are obvious downsides to brevity, on occasions, however if this form of communication gets various people to communicate, who would often not be so inclined, then surely this is a benefit.

All Twitter screenshots below are reproduced with permission of Twitter, Inc.

Twitter homepage may be found at http://twitter.com/

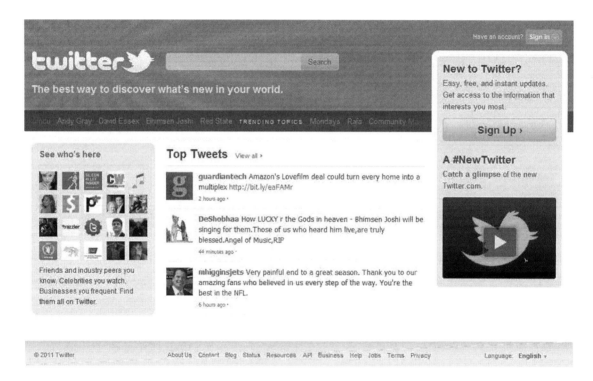

Twitter Explained Further

The Twitter About Us page has links to some good explanations about Twitter and may be found at http://twitter.com/about

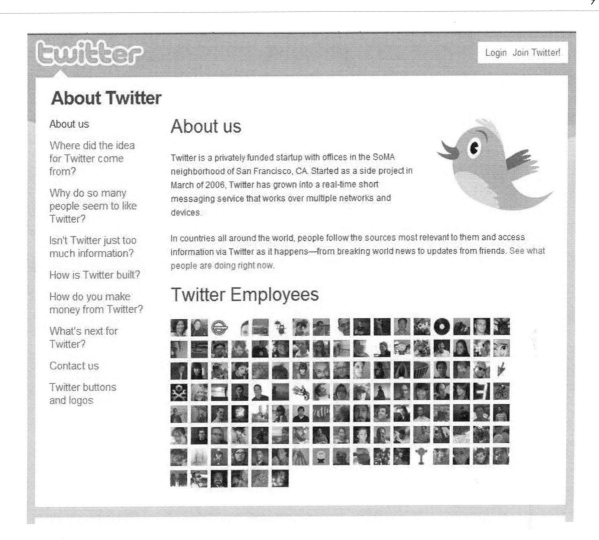

Profile Page Example

As an example of a profile page, go to my personal profile page at http://twitter.com/ aquinasrulz

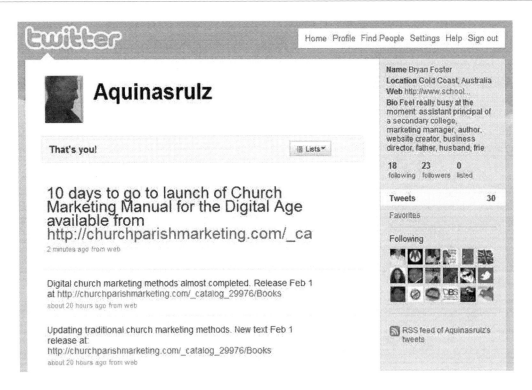

Home Page Sample

As an example of a Twitter homepage see my home page. This page is found at http://twitter.com/home

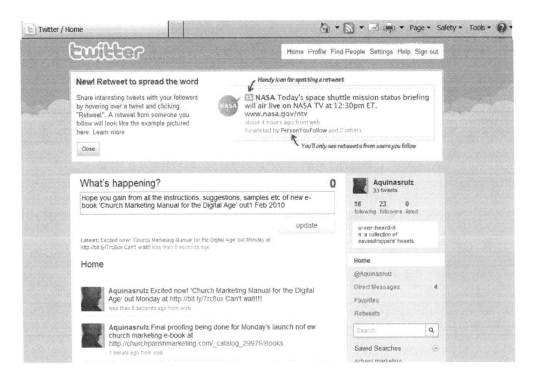

Privacy

I suggest you check out the Twitter Privacy statement before signing up. This statement is available at: http://twitter.com/privacy

Be aware that with all internet sites, especially social networking sites, your information may be seen by the general public. In certain circumstances viewing may be limited to selected people. Be fully aware of each website's Privacy and Terms and Conditions statements.

Sign Up

To commence a new Twitter account go to: https://twitter.com/signup

Twitter Groups

Be aware that Twitter Groups exist but are not a part of Twitter, Inc. itself. This may not suit your security or privacy concerns.

If you are interested in continuing to form a Twitter group go to http://twittgroups.com/confirm.php?oauth_token=d5G5hhEuJGJVY6cwtZjO9sMuqUtchAUfGtoLzTdltDs

This page details many of the group options available through this website.

You will need to then login to Twitter and continue the application process.

LinkedIn

This is a social networking website for professional people. It opens up the opportunity to engage with another group of parishioners and potential parishioners.

The same principles apply for use of this Social Networking Website as for the other previously explored.

Sign Up

To Sign Up go to: http://www.linkedin.com/

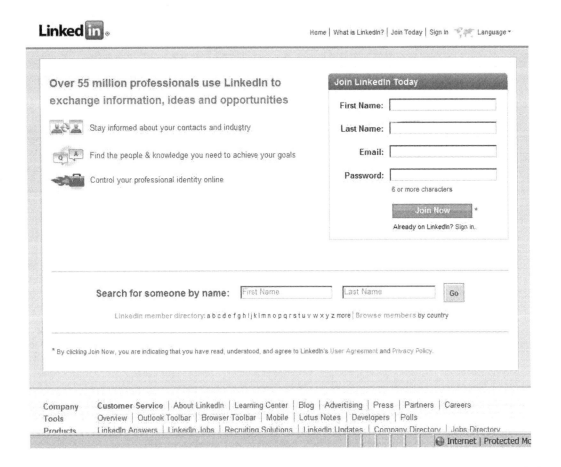

Sample Professional Page

A sample extract of my professional profile page is below and may be found at http://www.linkedin.com/myprofile?trk=hb_tab_pro

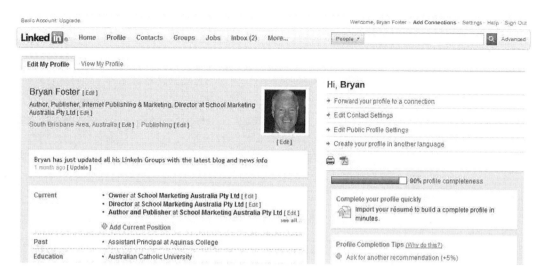

Form Groups for Discussion

There is also the option to form Groups for discussion purposes of topics relevant to the group. An example is my *Church Marketing and Parish Marketing* Group seen at http://www.linkedin.com/groupAnswers?viewQuestions=&gid=2242194&forumID=3&sik=1264051915108

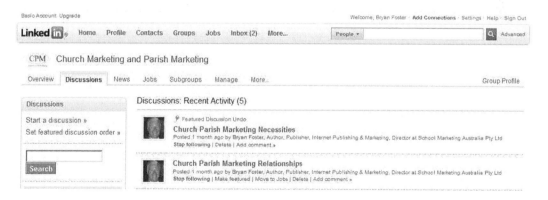

To create a group you will need to sign in and go to http://www.linkedin.com/createGroup?displayCreate=&trk=anet_creategrp Complete the form as requested and follow the prompts.

Privacy and Safety

Remember to read the User Agreement and Privacy.

Video Uploads

Uploading your church videos to your own parish website adds a special dimension for visitors to your site. You may also consider uploading these to other video storage sites for website flow increase + SEO advantages.

Uploading Video to Church Website

I have found the easiest method for this, which has a double advantage, is to upload the video to 'You Tube' and then embed the video from You Tube into my website. This was initially as a recommendation from my web-builders.

This is a relatively simple procedure, plus it has the added bonus of increasing your website's SEO profile and traffic to your website through your church website links you have placed on You Tube when uploading your video to You Tube.

Let us start by uploading a video to You Tube.

Uploading a Video to You Tube

Go to the You Tube homepage at http://www.youtube.com/ The appearance of this page varies continually as videos are uploaded. However, the basic template looks like the one below:

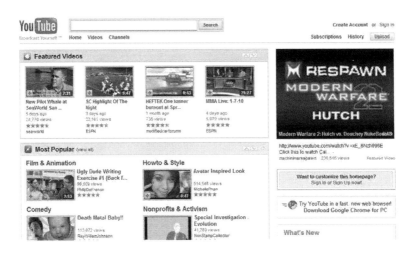

You will then need to click on the Create Account link in the top right hand corner and go to http://www.youtube.com/create_account:

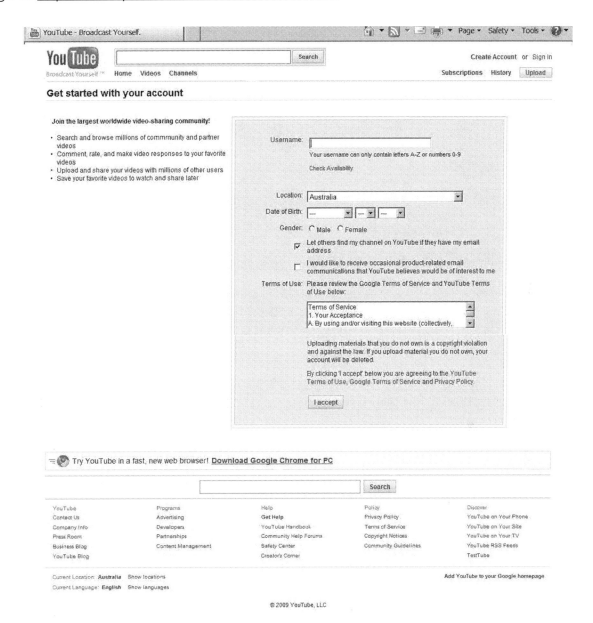

Complete the online form to create an account.

Then click on Upload and follow directions to upload a video.

The following screen will appear from http://upload.youtube.com/my_videos

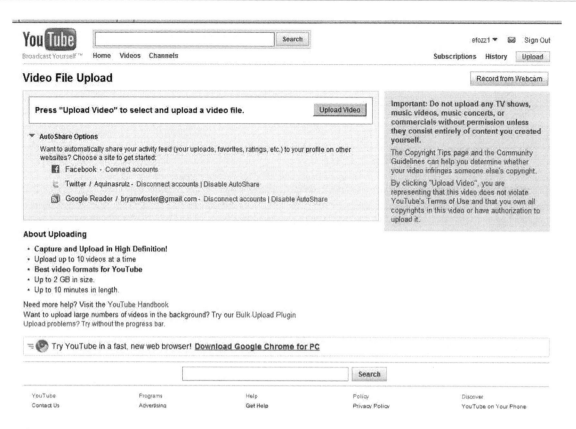

('Getting Started: Optimizing your video upload's on You Tube details the video specifi-
cations for best results at

http://www.google.com/support/youtube/bin/answer.py?answer=132460&topic=16612
&hl=en-US

These webpages are not shown in this e-book. It also may be of interest that this webpage above also details information on HD formatted videos, how best to upload wide-
screen videos.)

Continuing with Uploading videos.

Next click on 'Upload Video' and you will go to the webpage below at http://upload.
youtube.com/my_videos.

You will next need to select the video file from your computer. The uploading then
begins.

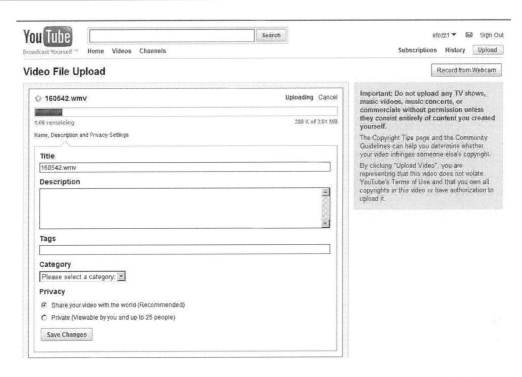

Next add a **Description,** in the Description box (see above image), of the video that is succinct and explains what the video is about and any purpose, etc needing to be stated.

Add **Tags** in the Tag box (see above image) similar as for Blogs i.e. a few key words and phrases that people might search for to discover your video in search engines. Select a Category and Privacy level.

Instructions to Embed Video

In your You Tube account open the video you want to embed on the You Tube site. (See an example below, which is from my You Tube account.)

Click on the star at the end of the 'Embed' box in the right column.

Tick appropriate boxes as needed. Often I don't tick the 'Include related videos' box, as I would just like my video showing and not the option of others being selected by You Tube to also become available to the viewer of your video.

Select a color border if preferred, as well as the size it is to be on your screen, by clicking over your choices.

Normally select one of the first two sizes.

Then highlight / select everything in the 'Embed box' as I have done in the sample below and Copy this.

The YouTube image below comes from http://www.youtube.com/watch?v=LHKcGUlhdlc

To embed the video on your website

Go to the management software for your website, then to the webpage that you want to embed the video on. Next you will need to go to the HTML section for that page. In my software I click on the HTML button at the bottom of the webpage I want to embed the video onto. You will see it at the bottom left below.

This takes me to the HTML script. I then find where I want the You Tube video embedded amongst all the text. In this particular case I look for the text with 'Methods – Strategies - Examples' (see below the image on the screen) because these are the words immediately before where the embedding will occur.

See the highlighted text below. This is the actual text I copied off You Tube for embedding and then pasted to my management site in the appropriate position on the webpage that I wanted the video to appear.

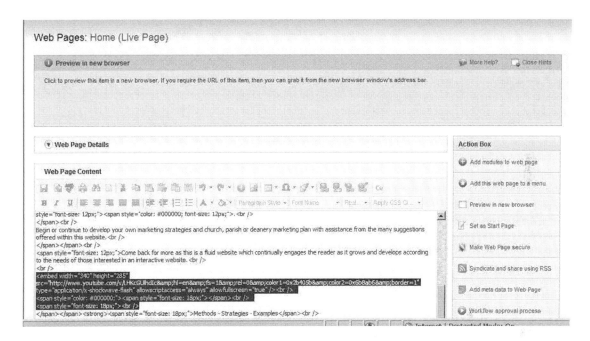

Save the page.

Check your website to see if the video is positioned as expected.

Repeat any of the processes as needed until all is correct.

You can also upload videos to other video storage websites apart from You Tube, such as *flickr* at http://www.flickr.com/ and *Daily Motion* at http://www.dailymotion.com/en.

The main reasons for this would be for:

- Search Engine Optimization or
- more traffic flow back through web-links to your church website.

Skype

Skype allows for free calls across the internet between account holders. It allows callers with webcam to see each other. Another great church marketing opportunity!

Why Skype as part of the church marketing plan?

Apart from it being another technology that involves some or many of our church goers / parishioners and that we need to meet these people where they are at, it is also:

- quite an exciting technological development
- one which should increase quite significantly in popularity over the short to mid-term.

People are going to enjoy:

- cost benefits, which are free for the basic webcam usage
- time saving benefits -
- possibly be more willing on occasions to get into conversations from home / work with the parish office personnel or other parishioners, than actually meet with these people
- seeing the people who they interact with over the 'phone' (webcam) through their computer.

Skype Explained

Skype account holders may make FREE calls to each other between two internet connected computers and also to view each other via webcam i.e. video cameras built-in or attached / placed externally to the computers.

There are also **various options which require a payment**. Explore the Skype site for these.

Skype's main options are: Free calls between account holders, video calls and instant messaging over the internet. Plus phone calls to phones anywhere in the world for a fee.

This section will emphasize the free calls option whereby callers over the internet get to see each other as they speak.

For full details go to: www.skype.com

Specifically for video calling details go to: http://www.skype.com/intl/en/allfeatures/videocall/

A reminder to also explore the Term and Polices at: http://www.skype.com/intl/en/legal

To download Skype press the 'Download' button at: http://www.skype.com/intl/en/download/skype/windows/

Below are the screens which will appear, at time of writing this text, as you progress through the Download. As part of the Download you will also be asked to '**Create a new Skype account**' as seen below.

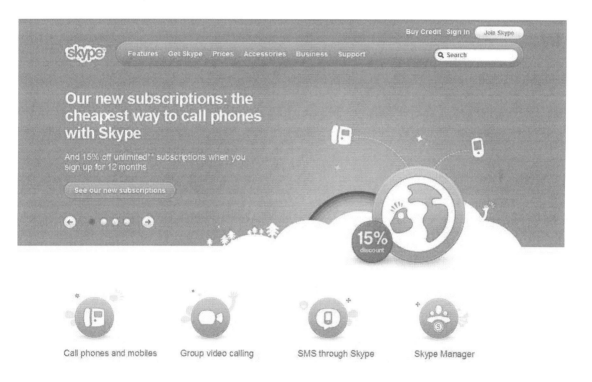

Buy Skype Credit · Sign in · Help · Search

Download **Use Skype** **Business** **Shop** **Account**

You're now downloading Skype

 The Skype download should start within seconds. If it doesn't, you can start download again. You need Windows® 2000, XP, Vista or 7 to run Skype.

How do I install Skype?

 Save the Skype Setup Application
A window will open asking what you want to do with a file called **SkypeSetup.exe**. Click 'Save File'.

Run the Skype Setup Application
When the download is complete, click on the SkypeSetup.exe. file from the Mozilla Downloads window to open the Skype Setup application. Alternatively, you can open it directly from the location you saved it, usually your desktop.

Follow the Setup Wizard
The Skype Setup Wizard will appear and guide you through the rest of the installation.

Launch Skype
 After the installation has finished, you can open Skype at any time by clicking the Skype icons located either on your desktop or in your system tray (this is the found at the bottom right of your screen).

For your computer
Windows
Windows (Business version)
Mac OS X
Linux

For your mobile
Windows Mobile
Nokia N800/N810
Nokia N900
Skype Lite
iPhone
Skype on PSP®

Skype built-in
WiFi phones
Cordless phones
3 Skypephone

Beta versions
Windows
Mac OS X

Toolbars for Skype
Skype Office Toolbar
Skype Email Toolbar

Your security on Skype
Learn how secure Skype is.

VoIP explained
Learn how VoIP works.

Related
o Free Skype-to-Skype calls
o Free video calls
o Add contacts
o Improve call quality
o Get help

No emergency calls with Skype. Skype is not a replacement for your ordinary telephone and can't be used for emergency calling.

International (English) About us Affiliates Jobs Rates Security Site map Privacy policy · Legal · © 2010 Skype Limited

Continue following the prompts to achieve an account membership and the successful download of the software needed to operate Skype.

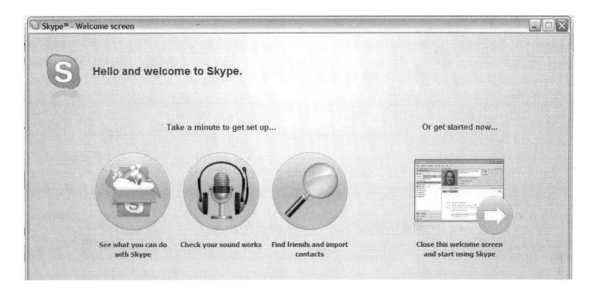

Enjoy this new and ever-expanding, inexpensive, very contemporary, communication option.

Build those church networks!

Chatting on the Web

by a Dad and his 15 year old

A most enjoyable experience was just had through discussing with my 15 year old the best use of chat rooms. Chat rooms are good for use with younger people, particularly for organizing something ...

Benefits of 'Chatting'

Below is an extract of the key points on the benefits of 'Chatting' ... in chat language... ordered as per our conversation:

- to talk to people
- plan events
- keep in contact
- sometimes good because it doesn't need to be saved
- can be saved if you want
- mainly for chats between singles but you can talk to more than one person at a time, if you're organizing something, for example
- better than emails for group chats

The most appropriate use for chat rooms would be when conversing with or via young people to make arrangements for something e.g. a social event, upcoming church celebration, etc,.

Chat Room for a Church

A simple way to implement this church chat room for young people would be to engage a young/er person who the youth of the parish relate to and have him / her act as an intermediary with those charged with making the arrangements for the upcoming activity. This person would be a leader of the youth.

The leader would need to arrange for the young people to:

- all be 'friends' (members of their chat line group) on the chat line
- chat at a particular time and day

- develop an agenda, but not need to be too formalized, but be capable of 'going with the flow'
- make all 'friends' in the chat feel welcome and valued
- be able to lead a chat respectfully so as to achieve outcomes – emphasis is on 'chat' and not a 'meeting'
- call follow-up chats as needed
- feedback to key people within the organizational structure of the church
- feedback to other young people who weren't involved
- feedback to parishioners the process and outcomes – a well informed parish is usually a supportive parish.

Sample Chat Room and Sign Up Process

Hotmail at Windows Live is a popular chat room for young people. This chapter will use Hotmail as the sample study.

Another popular chat room is at Yahoo (see http://messenger.yahoo.com/ for details).

To begin the sign up process for Windows Live (including Hotmail) go to:

http://login.live.com/login.srf?wa=wsignin1.0&rpsnv=11&ct=1263351950&rver=6.0.5285.0&wp=MBI&wreply=http:%2F%2Fmail.live.com%2Fdefault.aspx&lc=1033&id=64855&mkt=en-au

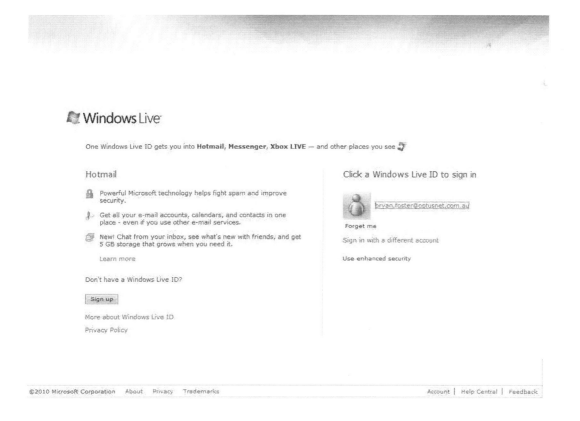

To find out more about the Hotmail click on 'Learn More' at the above site. This will take you to the screen below at http://mail.live.com/mail/about.aspx

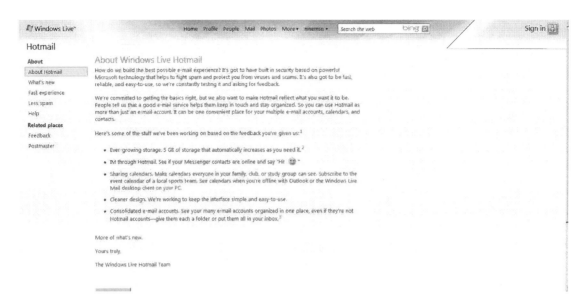

You can either continue with the Sign Up by clicking on the 'Sign up' button on the first screen above at http://login.live.com/login.srf?wa=wsignin1.0&rpsnv=11&ct=126 3351950&rver=6.0.5285.0&wp=MBI&wreply=http:%2F%2Fmail.live.com%2Fdefault. aspx&lc=1033&id=64855&mkt=en-au

or you may want to explore more about what Windows Live has to offer.

Overview of Windows Live Messenger

An overview of Windows Live Messenger (Hotmail is a part of this) may be found through the 'About' link at the very bottom of the page. This goes to http://download.live.com/

Here you will find much information about the options that Windows Live offers including:

- Messenger (Hotmail live chat – details follow in this text)
- Email
- Blogging – Writer
- Photos and Videos - editing and posting online – Photo Gallery and Movie Maker
- Web Browsing – Toolbar and Family Safety

All you do is go to this webpage and click on the links of interest. Attractive and informative pages appear. To find out more information, click on the links in the left hand column below the term 'Features'.

To download selected programs follow the instructions in the right hand column.

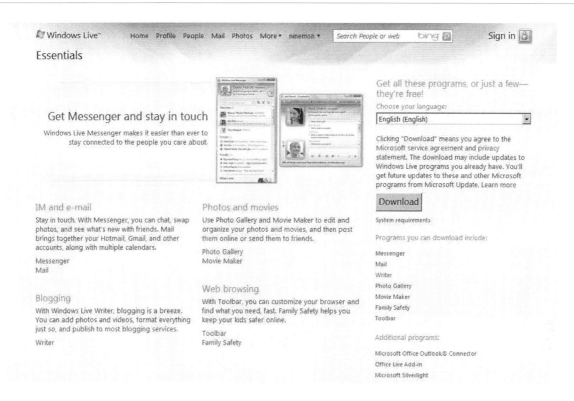

Click on 'Messenger' to get the general information webpage about the Chat option at http://download.live.com/messenger

This page has links to numerous areas of possible interest for you. You may like to explore these before proceeding.

Download Other Aspects of Windows Live

When ready Click on 'Download' and follow screen instructions.

Make sure you agree with the Microsoft service agreement and Privacy which are both found above the 'Download button' in the screen below or at the bottom of the following screen, the 'Create your Windows Live ID' screen.

Sign Up

To Sign Up and create your Windows Live ID for Hotmail go to the page below

https://signup.live.com/signup.aspx?ru=http%3a%2f%2fmail.live.com%2f%3frru%3dinbox&wa=wsignin1.0&rpsnv=11&ct=1263351950&rver=6.0.5285.0&wp=MBI&wreply=http:%2F%2Fmail.live.com%2Fdefault.aspx&lc=1033&id=64855&mkt=en-au&bk=1263351951&rollrs=12&lic=1

Windows Live™

Create your Windows Live ID

It gets you into all Windows Live services—and other places you see 🔗
All information is required.

ⓘ Already using **Hotmail**, **Messenger**, or **Xbox LIVE**? Sign in now

Windows Live ID:	[ ] @ [live.com.au ▾]
	[Check availability]
Create a password:	[ ]
	6-character minimum; case sensitive
Retype password:	[ ]
Alternate e-mail address:	[ ]
	Or choose a security question for password reset
First name:	[ ]
Last name:	[ ]
Country/region:	[Australia ▾]
State/Territory:	[Select one ▾]
Postal Code:	[ ]
Gender:	○ Male ○ Female
Birth year:	[Example: 1990]

SNGRBE

Characters:	[ ]
	Enter the 8 characters you see

☑ Send me e-mail with promotional offers and survey invitations from Windows Live, Bing, and MSN. (You can unsubscribe at any time.)

Clicking **I accept** means that you agree to the Microsoft service agreement and privacy statement.

[I accept]

0 Microsoft | Privacy | Legal   Help Central | Account | Feedba

Once you click the 'I accept' button above you go to your Hotmail Inbox which is shown below. Mine is at http://mail.live.com/?rru=inbox

Click on 'Getting started with Windows Live Hotmail' in the Inbox above. For my account the link took me to my account at http://mail.live.com/?rru=inbox

To avoid confusion between Windows live and Hotmail see the following comment which is taken from the screen below:

"Hotmail is part of Windows Live.

Your Hotmail address and password give you free access to all Windows Live services so you can stay connected with the people and things that matter to you. Share photos, write a blog, get 25 GB of free online storage, and more."

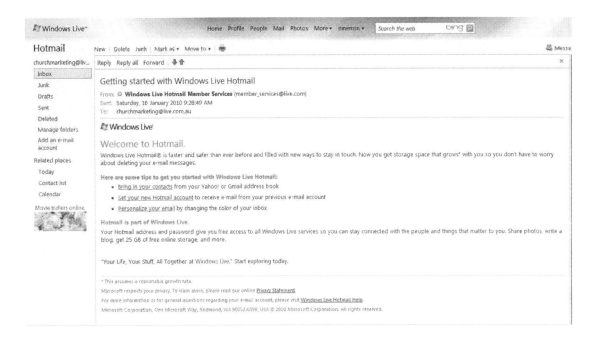

Another good Windows Live link is 'Get to Know Windows Live Hotmail' at http://www.windowslive-hotmail.com/LearnMore/

This webpage covers the topics:

- Personalize
- Protect
- Connect
- Organize
- Versatility
- Windows Live

Get Chatting

Once you have signed up, the Windows Live program will normally start when you open your computer. If it does not start automatically, then go to the toolbar on the bottom right of your screen. Click on the little person next to a green box (or wherever you have these toolbar placed) to open Windows Live. The screen which should appear is:

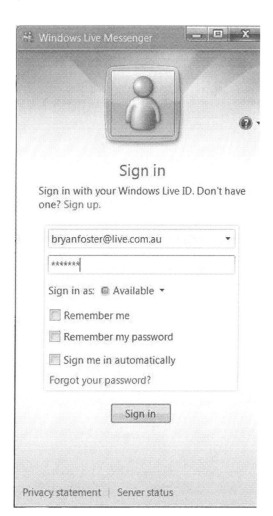

Next sign in your email address you used to sign up for this site plus your password and following the various prompts.

The first time you get connected a one-off screen will appear. It offers further assistance. Decide if you need to use its options or just close the window.

You will need to get 'friends' before you can begin chatting. Follow the instructions from this webpage.

Enjoy chatting, particularly in groups tasked with organizing events / activities!

Church Marketing Plan
Church Marketing Manager

Church Marketing Plan
Church Marketing Manager

The PLAN. The Manager. The spend. The support. The evaluation.

The right person managing the right marketing plan, being given a realistic budget and support and using continual evaluation techniques and feedback are high priorities for a successful marking plan within your church.

This chapter gets to the heart of these critical decisions. Often tough decisions need to be made and hopefully this section helps ease that concern.

Big or small budgets can both have varying degrees of success.

Know your market and its needs and develop plans accordingly.

A longer term plan often eases that initial budget constraint. Success often leads to more success. Decision makers become open to more appropriate budgets.

Headings

Church Marketing Plan Overview Sample

Church Marketing Manager
Church Marketing Manager Support Clusters
Branding
Budget
Church Surveys
Church Marketing Plan Evaluation
Deanery Marketing Plan (DMP)

Church Marketing Plan

A successful Church Marketing Plan (CPM) is critical to a successful parish!
Be well prepared!
Plan!

Church Marketing Plan Overview Sample

Define what you have to offer:

- vision and mission, personnel, sacramental / prayer life, pastoral and welfare support programs, schools, religious and pastoral education, facilities, etc
- specific ages and groups catered for - from infants to the elderly
- future plans – programs, staffing, facilities, etc

Define your target group:

- through surveys, observations, experience, gifts and talents available / needed
- proximity to / involvement with church educational institutes – elementary / primary, secondary and tertiary
- any expansion – programs, facilities, staffing

Budget:

- realistically support the church marketing plan
- be flexible and open to growth and change as the needs arise
- continually develop over time through needs and experiences

Personnel and talents available - including Church Marketing Manager

Select Marketing Strategies:

- Church Marketing Relationships
- Church Marketing Resources (include branding, advertising)
- Using the Media
    - * Internet and other Contemporary methods
    - * Both for Free (Media Releases / Editorial, etc) and for Fee (Advertising)

Evaluation

Analysis of the Church Marketing Plan

- **The Parish Priest is ultimately responsible for the CMP.**

- **The Church Marketing Plan is based on the parish's Vision and Mission Statement.**

- A CMP is the plan used to market the church / parish to the community. The community includes all people who know, or those who you want to know, about the church / parish. These include the general public in your catchment region, parishioners, potential parishioners, parish staff, church school staff, other schools' staff, present and past students, parents and aged care staff and guests.

- The CMP includes the strategies used within a defined budget.

- The plan is used to inform all stakeholders, and other targeted groups, of the benefits and successes of the church / parish.

- It also informs about aspects which may be of interest.

- It also needs to plan for issues which may arise of a controversial nature.

- The plan should inform and emphasize the real nature of the parish or the direction the parish is planning or presently implementing.

- A realistic budget is part of the CMP.

- Marketing is relatively inexpensive when viewed in the terms of the potential gains made – reputation, new parishioners, supportive present parishioners, enrolments at its schools, etc.

- The CMP can benefit from the combination of views of staff and others associated with the parish community.

- In the initial stages of developing the parish's first real plan it is often best to include a variety of interest groups for gaining ideas and suggestions about how best to market your parish. These thoughts may then be used as felt necessary.

- The Parish Priest needs input and has the overall responsibility to implement the plan.

CMP Evaluation

The CMP should be evaluated at least yearly and appropriate adjustments made for the following year. Changes may need to be made throughout the year depending on changing circumstances.

A CMP is not...

A successful Church Marketing Plan is a lot more than the Church's stationery and news-letter.

It should avoid 'dressing-up' the parish in a way which cannot be supported.

Be ethical ...

Apart from being unethical, more than likely, any unethical aspects would eventually become apparent as being incorrect to the stakeholders and others.

This would have an adverse impact on the parish's reputation and hence parishioners' and community's involvement.

Who needs a Church Marketing Plan?

All churches need a Church Marketing Plan.

Informing the community is seen by most parishes to be an important aspect of their ministry and mission. **It also leads to the best promoters of the church / parish.**

A CMP may be as simple or as complex as needed to achieve the desired outcomes.

The plan is needed whether:

- a church / parish presently has a large parishioner base or
- it is about to re/open or
- it is losing parishioners.

**The best time to market a church / parish is when it is successful.
At this stage there are so many approaches which may be taken to highlight the benefits.**

However, it usually becomes an issue when parishioner numbers are dropping or when a new church is opening need by. At this stage a specifically targeted program is required. Don't be caught out!

Church Marketing Manager

Overview

The Parish Priest will often delegate this Church Marketing Manager (CMM) role to a parish staff member or parishioner.

Full-time, Part-time or shared? The PP decision...

However, it is best not to lose sight of employing the best person for this position.

The Church Marketing Manager will be responsible for the Church Marketing Plan and responsible to the Parish Priest.

Full / Part-Time or Shared Role

Most CMMs would be part time in this position these days. Budgetary restraints would basically necessitate this. These people would combine this role with their other primary role, usually that of Parish Manager or Parish Secretary.

To share the role, I believe, could be detrimental to it. Having someone knowing everything there is to know about was has occurred, is being planned for and involved with the future implementation of the Church Marketing Plan is a definite advantage.

I feel that the time is coming when an individual church or at least a combination of churches within a certain region / religious order / deanery will employ a full-time CMM.

CMM Skills Needed

The person who takes on this role will need to:

- be interested in the area of marketing and preferably passionate about it

- be a person of integrity

- be able to base the CMP on the parish's Vision and Mission statement

- be aware of the marketing needs of a particular parish

- have good interpersonal skills

- be able to build professional relationships with key stakeholders, members of the media and various local business personnel

- have a creative flare and appreciation of what 'catches the eye' of the targeted audiences

- have good literary skills

- have good computer skills, particularly with creative AV software packages, or at least an appreciation of these along with other staff members or parishioners who would implement the software packages under your direction

- have a good appreciation of the internet and be able to implement all that this means of communication offers your particular church

- be capable of developing and implementing a viable budget

- be keen to learn and develop more successful forms of marketing and marketing skills.

Church Response to CMM

The church personnel will need to:

- be open to various forms of marketing

- be willing to try other strategies, particularly successful strategies from different parishes and schools

- provide an appropriate budget to allow for the broadness and depth needed for the implementation of a successful CMP

- give appropriate time to the CMM to develop and implement the CMP

- support the CMM in this difficult area

- give time to the CMM for professional development to gain appropriate or advanced skills to implement the CMP

- have access to specialist IT personnel who may be needed to assist with various aspects of the role.

Support Clusters

All CMMs need support no matter their perceived proficiency or experience.

Overview

One of the best forms of support cluster may include each church's CMM, Parish Priest, Pastoral Associate and members of the Parish Pastoral Council.

Another support is a cluster of CMMs, usually within local proximity.

Either support cluster could benefit from inviting input from other specialists be they from other parishes and schools, diocesan authorities, school employing authorities or other consultants. Input on current marketing practices for within that cluster and / or by offering suggestions for improvement would be beneficial.

Support Cluster - Church Leadership Team

The Parish Priest should always be an integral part of any CMP.

The Parish Priest, along with the church's Leadership Team, would be a wonderful support structure for the CMM.

To have gifted people literally within earshot of one another and able to have ideas bounced off each other, and opinions and ideas shared, would be beneficial.

The Parish Priest and Leadership Team should have confidence in the CMM and allow this person to develop the CMP without interference. This, however, needs to be done in consultation with the Parish Priest and maybe also with the other school Leadership Team members.

The CMM would initially need to gain the trust of the Parish Priest and Leadership Team. Time, professional development and experience of successfully completing and implementing a CMP may be integral to gaining this support.

Support Clusters of CMMs

Often CMMs feel that all churches and parishes, even those of the same denomination, are rivals.

This is most likely far from the truth.

The more similar churches and parishes work together, in this case from the marketing perspective, the more proficient and successful each one should be.

It is believed that the old adage is correct: 'The star team is better than a team of stars'.

Regular meetings of CMMs, where successful and non-successful strategies of marketing are discussed and possible solutions espoused would be of benefit to each church or parish involved.

These meetings could also include shared creative thinking time on possible strategies along with resource development for each particular church or parish.

Diocesan Support and Deanery Clusters

Diocesan support would be available to many churches and parishes. This may be done on a one to one basis i.e. the parish and diocesan personnel, or as a deanery cluster of parishes along with diocesan personnel.

Using the combined expertise of the diocese and deanery, along with any budgetary assistance, could be of substantial value to each church or parish.

The diocese would most likely employ experienced marketing people and journalists.

The diocese may be able to supply a budget to assist parishes, particularly those in need.

The initial onus may be on parishes to approach the diocesan Communication and Marketing Manager. Be clear with your proposed needs or queries.

A first time CMM may make this approach early on to gain initial momentum and advice. They may also gain financial support to kick start the marketing process.

Once the process has begun these CMMs could use the other support structures mentioned above plus resources like this text for guidance and assistance.

Branding

Branding is often a person's first contact with the church. It is usually a visual image seen. It may also be a verbal input.

> Branding's importance must not be underestimated. First impressions do count!

First Impressions

The first impression may be gained from the following:

- Website design

- Welcome by office staff / Office decor etc

- Prospectus / Information Pack cover, pages and inclusions

- Uniform of office staff

- Stationery received

- e-Newsletter or newsletter design and front page content

- Telephone call response by office staff / voicemail response / dedicated line for mass times recording, upcoming events, etc

- White and Yellow pages listings

- Advertisement in newspaper or magazine, radio, etc

- Flyer

- Student or staff at parish schools

- Reputations of parish and schools as espoused from someone within the community

The branding of the parish needs to be well considered and representative of the parish's vision and mission. It needs to show how the parish is to be seen within the community.

Uniformity

Branding needs uniformity to be a powerful, positive tool.

Mixing and matching branding causes a weak and disjointed image to be apparent.

This is to the disadvantage of the parish in a number of ways. The confusing images distract and hence do not leave the desired impact.

The parish may be seen itself as disjointed and 'not together' and hence causing various follow-up difficulties.

Key Branding Areas

- **Key <u>primary areas</u> of branding** include:

    - Colors
    - Logo / emblem
    - Motto / Catch phrase
    - Uniform design
    - Graphics and page layout
    - Key words to epitomize the church

Colors may vary according to the purpose i.e. outside colors of the church / parish centre may differ to the inside colors and these may differ from stationery and advertising colors.

To have the same colors everywhere can become overbearing. However, there would be less of a difficulty with soft plain colors but these colors often aren't strong enough for stationery and advertising.

It is important though that those colors selected for each area, inside and outside, along with stationery and advertising are simple, matching and constant throughout that particular usage.

- These following areas then form the basis for the **secondary areas of branding**, including:

    - Stationery design, which would include page graphics and layouts of parish details

- Logo and motto inclusion on uniforms

- Website design

- e/i-Newsletter and Newsletter design

- Covers and page layouts for parish produced information booklets and brochures (e/i-booklets, e/i-flyers and e/i-brochures)

- Advertisement designs, including for the media, as well as posters, flyers, booklets

- Layout of front office

- Welcoming introduction for telephone answering / voicemails

- Welcoming at office front counter

- Parish DVD / CD graphics

- Key verbal phrases for radio, DVD / CD and telephone on-hold

- The following form the basis for **tertiary use of branding**, including:

  - How the various secondary forms will be used

  - Various combinations of secondary for

Branding Changes

> **Evaluation of primary, secondary and tertiary branding forms is essential.**

Branding needs to be thoroughly considered as it is imperative to maintain the overall branding and most specific forms for a period of years.

Major changes with branding should not occur at least for three to five years (unless the initial branding failed).

The successful images created and regularly reinforced within the minds of people from the branding are highly valuable. Think of major brands that seem to be almost eternal e.g. McDonald's and Coca Cola.

Parishes are by no means within this category for financial outlay, outside consultants or market-share, however with good branding each church and parish is a small

microcosm and capable of being every bit as successful within its own demographic as the large corporations.

> Changes may be needed within any specific branding period if some aspects of branding have found to be unsuccessful.

Changes will usually cause large amounts of wasted time, resources and funding.

> It is best to be wise before the event.

Creativity of Design

Seeking advice from other successful churches and schools, or in some cases consultants for these churches and schools, is a very good start.

Try to be original as much a possible, within your own market!

It is best not to 'copy', or be too similar to, other parish's or schools' branding.

By all means take those aspects which would suit your particular parish and adapt these to your particular needs.

However, parishes may benefit from similarities with parishes and schools both in and not in their own region.

A uniformity of theme within a region or religious order can work well when done properly and with the correct appreciation of the 'market'.

> **… with good branding, each parish is a small microcosm and capable of being every bit as successful within its own demographic as the large corporations…**

Budget

A successful Church Marketing Plan needs a well funded budget

Mmm … Money time!

This is probably the most controversial aspect of any CMP.

Overview

Various people within each church community have differing views on the amount which should be afforded to the Church Marketing Budget (CMB).

Parish Priests and Parish Managers need to be aware that the implementation of a good CMP would inevitably drive up community engagement and parishioner numbers!

In today's dollar values spending $20 - $40000 on an average parish's CMB would be a good investment.

This would need to be proportionately reviewed according to overall parish budget, the number of parishioners and the overall need of the parish to build and maintain parishioner numbers.

When the CMP is being developed for a specified year, key stakeholders, particularly the Parish Priest, Parish Manager and the CMM, need to assess the budget requirements.

The budget will have a significant impact on a CMP for any year.

The budget includes all areas of the CMP which incur expenses.

Invest During Good Times

Good times are the best times to invest. This enables the parish's reputation to be enhanced considerably.

Resting on the laurels of the past can become an expensive exercise when the reputation is forgotten or when a new challenge comes from other competing interests, including other churches and distractions within society.

Shared CMPs – Regionalized or Localized

> Shared CMPs across a number of parishes may be another way of efficiently budgeting.

This could be **regionalized** e.g.:

- a combined deanery budget to be shared amongst parishes or
- a DMM (Deanery Marketing Manager) implementing the whole marketing plan for the deanery and individual parishes which are only required to develop their own essentials such as newsletters.

Or it may be a number of **localized parishes** working together and sharing the budget.

A shared budget may see different parishes marketing specific aspects for the cluster e.g.

- one may concentrate on Adult Education within the cluster
- another may market the varying sorts of prayer and liturgy on offer and differing times for each
- another may emphasize the welfare and social justice aspects within the cluster.

For some parishes this may be the only way to begin marketing or to maintain a CMP in any form what-so-ever.

Caution

Even though this may appear to save financially, it takes away from the individual uniqueness of each parish.

Marketing is often more successful when emphasizing a uniqueness.

Surveys

Surveys are often a good way to discover the views and needs of various stake-holders and of prospective parishioners.

Aims and Sample Questions

If the surveyed group believes that they will be listened to, and that the survey isn't an onerous one, then a greater percentage of quality responses will occur.

Simple questions will often elicit the best results.

Sample questions might be:

- What do you like best about (name) church / parish?
- What improvements could be made?
- Other suggestions?

Other more explicit questions could be asked, and depending on the audience, may be of benefit, however, in most cases it is best to KIS (Keep It Simple).

Feeder Schools

Surveying the various feeder schools of a particular church should point the parish in the right direction. The views of staff, parents and students of the schools are an invaluable aid as to how the parish is perceived and of areas needing improvement.

Discussion Groups

Following the survey, or in addition to the survey, Discussion Groups are often beneficial. Key stakeholders form the group/s.

Select an experienced facilitator / chairperson.

Be open to frank discussion. Be accommodating and respectful.

You will most likely need to make it clear that you are open to considering all views but the final decisions rest with the Parish Priest.

Varied responses will be inevitable.

It is the Parish Priest's and CMM's role to rank order responses and take on board those which are relevant and practical.

Survey vs. CMP Evaluation

These surveys are in addition to the CMP Evaluation.

The Survey is concentrating on the perceived strengths and weaknesses of the parish itself.

The CMP Evaluation is evaluating the church's marketing plan for that year.

The Surveys are held as needed.

The CMP Evaluation is best conducted at the same time of the any year. This may be midyear and away from the major church or sacramental events.

Church Marketing Plan Evaluation

The CMP needs to be evaluated yearly.

Stakeholders

Representatives from the Key Stakeholders groups within the parish need to give input.

These people would include:

- Parish Priest and priests
- Parish Manager
- Pastoral Associate
- Staff (as decided in consultation with PP)
- Parishioner representatives
- School Principals, Leadership Teams and student leaders
- Media Representatives (usually media contacts of yours and advertising consultants you dealt with, as needed)
- Diocesan and Deanery representatives as needed

Survey and Feedback

Feedback quantity and quality will vary.

Requested replies would be from both specific and general groups, for example, you may target specific groups of parishioners e.g. Parish Pastoral Council and School Board, but also invite interested parishioners through the parish's and schools' newsletters to respond.

A simple questionnaire sent to these people asking three questions will often give enough detail for a fair appraisal and follow-up discussion with the parish leadership team and CMM.

The questions could be:

- The CMP for [Parish Name] for this year was successful in what ways?
- The CMP for [Parish Name] for this year was lacking in what ways?
- How would you suggest the CMP for [Parish Name] be adjusted for next year?

The CMM would then summarize these responses in an honest way and present the views to the parish's Leadership Team.

It is also good to include specific examples from each question from key people e.g.

- a Mothers' Group may be the only ones aware of specific children or family needs;
- a Principal may be the only one who is aware of issues regarding visitations or parish involvement in his / her school or
- the Pastoral Associate may see specific pastoral issues in a particular light.

It is important that this isn't lost in the summary.

Others may like to develop a **survey which ranks specific statements** about the CMP from 5 to 1. The number of statements in the survey would need to be minimal to gain a good percentage of replies.

This type of survey would more than likely achieve a greater number of responses, yet the detail is limited. You may like to try a greater number of statements for groups or individuals you feel are more likely to respond.

You may also like to include a section for written responses to questions similar to the above three.

CMM Support

It is important that the CMM is supported by all groups to continue on the successful way or make various changes to improve.

Most common changes are made each year in the approach and / or forms of marketing used in each subsequent year. This is normal and leads to a more successful CMP each year.

Deanery Marketing Plan

> Combined marketing for individual regions could benefit each parish in that region.

Overview

Each parish needs its own CMP and the right to implement it free from outside interference.

However, each parish could also benefit from a Deanery Marketing Plan (DMP).

This plan may be one that encompasses all, or a selection of parishes, within the deanery.

The Deanery Marketing Plan would be a means of sharing ideas, costs and expertise.

The deanery's Parish Priests and CMMs should meet to plan the best approach, including budget, roles, timeline, branding, etc.

> **The stronger the overall deanery group of parishes is seen within that community, the stronger each individual parish is often seen.
> There is strength in numbers.**

Approaches could include emphasizing each parish's strength within the deanery.

Advantages

It also often happens that when a parish, which is perceived as more popular by sections of the community, is part of the DMP, each parish gains from that perception.

The perceived popular parish would not lose from this exposure because of its initial strength, along with it being seen as part of a strong viable network of like-minded parishes.

The deanery approach needs to account for the special needs, successes and expertise of a deanery and hence the parishes within that region, for a more successful DMP in that region.

Caution

Even though this may appear to save financially, it takes away from the individual uniqueness of each parish.

Marketing is often more successful when emphasizing a uniqueness.

Church Marketing Relationships

Church Marketing Relationships

One of the most successful forms of marketing can be quite low cost depending on the ability of the parish to get out there and be seen.

The power of the stakeholder must never be underestimated.

Word of mouth rules. The skill is in getting the right words spoken by the stakeholders!

Building relationships within the parish, with the schools and parish groups, is essential for a successful and welcoming church.

But don't be shy! Giving your stakeholders and other interested people the facts to back your parish and for them to want to be involved, is very important!

Parish Open Days, Recognition events and engaging with the schools through School Visitations are all integral to success.

Let them go away WANTING to 'tell the world' all those great things the world needs to hear about your church!

Headings

Powerful Stakeholders
Parish Open Day
Church-School Relationships
Feeder School Visitation
Taster Days
Parish Recognition Night / Parish Dinner

Powerful Stakeholders

The most powerful marketing influence in any Church is the parishioners and parish or school staff.

To have a successful Church Marketing Plan (CMP) the stakeholders need to be supportive of the Church and Parish.

Insiders' Views

The power of the insiders' voices to the local community is paramount. Society will more often place a remarkable amount of credit upon those who have an insider's perspective.

The views expressed by those directly involved within the church / parish will be their personal perceptions, sometimes correct, at other times not fully informed.

In some cases negative views could be deliberately espoused as truth, for some political or retributive cause. There is an inherent need to keep the insiders informed and accountable.

Diplomacy

The Parish Priest, Priests, School Principals, Leadership Teams, and Staffs need to be fully supportive of the vision and mission of the parish. They need to be diplomatic in their discussions with fellow parishioners and the community at large.

Confidence in the Church and Parish

The Parish Pastoral Council, Parish Committees, Parish Groups, School Boards and Parents and Friends / Citizens Associations and other key interest groups should be as fully informed as possible and able to see that the parish is working efficiently and fairly for all concerned.

These groups need to see that policies exist and are implemented, particularly relating to any foreseen difficulty.

Often perceptions need to be corrected through diplomacy and an openness showing that the parish is working for everyone's best interest in the best way possible for a parishioner or school environment.

All parishes have areas of concern, just like any other organization, yet they need to be allowed to sort out any difficulties and challenges.

Parishioners require certainty that problems will be addressed professionally and in the best interests of those involved.

The parish's reputation is paramount!

Families and individual parishioners need confidence in the policies, processes, strategies and endeavors of their parish.

The community at large is usually either ambivalent or wish for churches and parishes to be successful environments for their parishioners. Often society will be reluctant to support the church / parish if this success is not being met.

When the parish's main stakeholders, its parishioners, are pleased with the parish, the CMP is well on the way to success.

> **The CMP is then able to highlight all of the parish's vision and mission with authority. Its credibility will be high.**

Never underestimate the power of the stakeholder! A recent Nielsen Global Survey also found this to be the case. In the church's case the consumers are the parishioners.

Nielsen Survey Results and Extrapolation

"Despite the ever-expanding array of advertising platforms and sources, consumers around the world still place their highest level of trust in other consumers, according to a recent global Nielsen Internet survey.

Conducted twice-a-year among 26 486 internet users in 47 markets from Europe, Asia Pacific, the Americas and the Middle-East, Nielsen most recently surveyed consumers on their attitudes toward thirteen types of advertising – from conventional newspaper and television ads to branded websites and consumer-generated content.

The Nielsen survey found that overall, consumers trust other consumers above all else! 78% of respondents said they trusted – either completely or somewhat – the recommendation of other consumers."

('Word of Mouth' the most powerful selling tool: Nielsen Global Survey, 2007, The Nielsen Company, on http://www.nielsenmedia.com.au/news.asp?newsID=348)

"The Nielsen survey found that while new platforms like the Internet are beginning to catch up with older media in terms of ad revenues, traditional advertising channels continue to retain the public's trust.

(http://au.acnielsen.com/site/Trustinadvertising.shtml)

If we see parishioners as consumers of what churches offer, and that they and the general public react similarly to how they do with everyday products, we could extrapolate that people in general, be they parishioners or members of the general public, trust parishioners (for general public) and other parishioners (for parishioners) above all else when critiquing or evaluating a particular church or parish.

> **That is – parishioners are the greatest, trusted promoters of their particular church.**

Parish Open Day

An Open Day is a highly visible hands-on approach to introduce prospective parishioners and school children, their families and the community to the parish and schools.

Aim to involve all groups / institutes within the church for greatest success!

Overview

An effective Parish Open Day would include the parish, schools (including pre-school) and aged care facilities (if appropriate) simultaneously holding their Open Days if the venues are within the same precinct or close by each other.

This would encourage the flow through of people to all aspects of the parish over the half day +.

A parish conducting its own open day may be challenged in the number of new people it could draw.

Reasons for attendance

People attend for numerous reasons including:

- To view and appraise a potential parish and / or school for their family and child/ren

- To confirm or possibly change views they previously held

- To reconfirm the reasons they previously became parishioners or enrolled their child/ren at the school

- To support the parish and / or school in its public presentation

- To be active participants on the day with display stands, hospitality, etc

- To support their child/ren who have a particular part to play on the day e.g. band, choir or dramatic presentations, uniform parade, stall assistance, etc

- To see what the 'parish and / or school up the road' has to offer the neighborhood.

The Open Day is also open to members of the public. A well presented Open Day will cause varying degrees of public discussion over time.

Strategies

The marketing strategy for an Open Day may include:

- Flyers delivered to houses within the parish's and schools' catchment areas

- Posters – in large sizes for display in shopping centers, churches and school offices and around the school. (The parish and school community need to feel a part of any major event and promote it in their own way e.g. talking at home or to friends.)

- Producing a glossy parish magazine of 12-16 pages for distribution through the feeder schools for the secondary school, churches, group centers and the schools, etc

- Advertising in a selection of the local newspapers and magazines

- Advertising on a local radio station (The advertising would include key activities and times. A visit by radio station personnel on the day is a well received bonus but costs more.)

- Media releases and phone calls to key media people to try and get media to the event

- Sample bags on the day, which include various Parish Information Kits, paraphernalia, school prospectus, parish school DVDs, etc

- Balloons handed out on the day, as well as part of the curriculum and display sections, with the parish or school logos, in the parish or school colors e.g. 50/50 red and blue, and opposite colored ribbons

- Meeting and greeting by parishioners and student leaders

- Tours of the parish and schools, lead by parishioners and student leaders. School student leaders need to be in immaculately presented uniforms with identity badges.

- Stands within each precinct i.e. church grounds / parish centre, schools and aged facilities, etc to highlight particular aspects of the parish e.g.

- * Pastoral care
- * Prayer and sacramental / liturgical life
- * Groups and committees
- * Aged Care and Pre-School facilities and activities
- * Curriculum stands for all subject areas
- * Displays from different curriculum departments e.g. IT, Math, Industrial Skills, Hospitality
- * Opening of rooms, classrooms and classes to visitors

- Performances by parish musical groups / choirs, drama and music students etc

- Sporting activities

- Competitions e.g. chess, debates and sports' games

- Continual running of looped parish and school DVDs and other PowerPoints throughout the whole parish precinct

- Addresses by Parish Priest, Principal, Directors, Parish and School representatives and School Captains – these maybe at one presentation venue or separately if each aspect of the parish would like to operate individually

- Uniform Fashion Parades done in a contemporary and appealing style

For the staged event it is important that all the marketing is targeted to the staged event's theme e.g. Open Day.

Promotional Materials

Key personnel from the parish, schools, aged care facilities, etc would need to decide the best approach for promotional material:

- one set of themed promotional material for all entities within the parish or
- individual promotional material or
- a combination, often general parish material + individual institutional material
- (Numerous options are offered throughout this e-book)

Best time

The selected time would need to be appropriate so as to attract the largest number of targeted visitors.

A balance between the different aspects of the Open Day needs to be achieved.

It is often desirable for the public to have the opportunity to see students in action, yet this would be one of many foci. If this was the aim, a good time could be a Friday from 2pm to 5:30pm.

This allows for an hour of open classrooms where best teaching practice and resources should be on view.

Displays, performances and addresses could go from 3pm until 5:30pm

If there are difficulties with students, or open classrooms aren't considered a worthwhile marketing tool, then after school or weekend open days would be more appropriate.

Venues

How much of the parish facilities should be opened up to the public? Each venue would have their own ideas on this; however there are some guidelines which may assist:

- Open areas which would be of interest to potential parishioners, students and parents
- Open areas which highlight particular stand-out physical aspects
- Use your specialists to demonstrate those particular areas e.g.
  - Church, Parish Centre, Parish Office, Meeting Rooms, Meditation Room
  - Science and Computer laboratories, Wireless Computers, Industrial Skills, Hospitality and Restaurant, Sport, Performing and Fine Arts, Dance
  - Accommodation Rooms, Boarding Rooms, Aged Care Facilities, Therapy Rooms, Heated Therapy Pool, Entertainment Rooms, Dining Facilities, Car Parking
- Have an easily accessible, central, well lit area for display boards and display tables, which will allow for electrical connections for laptops and data projectors
- Use as many of the standout facilities for classes or demonstrations.

Uniformity

Uniformity of displays in line with the each institute's branding style is needed throughout that particular area.

The display stands, where possible, also need the same display board and table types for uniformity.

A number of parishioners, students and staff should be rostered to assist on each stand. Visitors enjoy talking to staff, students and the aged (within reason and where necessary under supervision).

Students should be immaculately dressed in school or performance uniform / costume.

Staff should be dressed in appropriate dress; often this would be semiformal depending on weather conditions and the image of parish and schools.

Addresses

Addresses need to be well prepared, succinct and supported by the best quality A/V possible. Using the parish's and / or school's facilities will highlight the technical equipment and its use to the visitors.

Parishioner and Parental Involvement

It is important to have parishioner and parental involvement. This may be through their expertise at various stands, acting as ushers, etc, or as is often the case, through providing afternoon tea throughout the afternoon, along with wine and cheese towards the end.

Church - School Relationships

> *Good relationships existing between the church and its school/s is in itself an outstanding marketing strategy.*

Improved Church – School Relationships

When the school communities speak positively about, and engage with, the parish, this enhances the parish considerably.

For best results for the parish it would generally be the **parish personnel who need to be the driving force** in building this relationship.

Church Leadership

This initially needs the full support of the Parish Priest, Principals, Pastoral Associate, Pre-School Director, Aged Care Director, Group Leaders, etc.

These leaders need to develop the support amongst their leadership teams and staff.

The school leadership team and staff would need to actively encourage student participation within the parish.

Parish Priests need to encourage their Principals and staff to offer suggestions on how to develop this relationship better.

Parish Engagement

Some suggestions for the parish:

Priests

- Priests need to be engaged and seen within the schools as much as possible e.g.

    * at school assemblies
    * staff morning teas
    * meeting students around the school grounds with teachers

(Don't fear this! Students generally enjoy this and gain considerably from it. With a teacher's assistance it would be a pleasant experience once the students accept that your interest and presence is legitimate.)

* school / year level / class masses or other liturgies
* as guest speakers within Religious Education classes
* attending pastoral care visits with the students to hospitals, street retreats for the homeless, aged care visitations and Prep classes
* attending Parents and Friends meetings and Board meetings
* presenting at School Information Nights, Open Days, Graduation.

- **Parish – School Liturgies and Groups**

It is through these engagements that relationships can develop e.g.

* Student / staff / priest liturgy groups to plan and celebrate weekly / fortnightly / monthly youth Eucharists. This would include students being involved with as much of the Eucharist as possible, including playing and leading the singing and music
* Parish / School Youth Groups
* Parish / School Social Justice Groups
* Parish / School student / young people retreats and reflection days
* Parish / School Street Retreats, usually at night
* Parish / School e/i-Newsletters / Newsletters for youth and families.

- **Other Key Church Personnel Engagement**

* Other key parish personnel, particularly the Pastoral Associate, need engagement with the school along similar lines as the priests but according to their areas of expertise e.g.
* Pastoral Associate being of assistance, but not in charge of, various sacramental, prayer or pastoral activities within the school
* Age Care Director supporting the visitations by students and addressing assemblies on the benefits of these visits
* Parishioners assisting particular classes or students as the need arises e.g.

  - retired trades-people or interested parishioners assisting with Hospitality or Industrial Skills classes
  - retired business or IT people assisting with these subjects, etc
  - other subject areas
  - coaching sporting teams
  - rehearsing students for Drama, Musicals, etc.

- **Improved School – School Relationships within the Parish**

When each school speaks positively about the other school, both schools' reputations are enhanced.

Strategies to Build Stronger School – School Relationships

Stronger relationships between the parish schools are formed through a variety of ways.

Some examples are:

- Staff professional gatherings e.g. curriculum development for primary years to middle years to senior years

- Staff professional gatherings for discussion regarding student levels for primary students going into secondary school, or junior school into middle school, or middle school into senior school

- Staff spiritual gatherings e.g. Beginning Year Eucharist, Prayer Afternoons (before a social event)

- Staff social involvement with each other e.g. gatherings shared across campuses

- Secondary students:
    * assist some primary classes or
    * share their creations e.g. art, writings, with selected classes / groups from their primary feeder school/s or
    * a Year 12 Day occurs when the Year 12 students are involved in a number of interest areas for a morning with the primary students e.g. sport, art, reading, drama, dance, etc, on a rotational basis

- Secondary students and staff assist with primary school events e.g. Fete, Liturgies

- Primary students attend Taster Days at the secondary school

- Primary students are involved with the secondary school's Open Day, Musical, etc

- Parental involvement e.g.
    * combined P&F / P&C associations and School Boards meet regularly
    * each school's Principal and key staff attend / address the other school's P&F and School Boards regularly
    * parents are invited to key events at the other school e.g. Musicals, Open Days, Fetes, Sports' Finals
    * parents with particular talents in required areas are invited to address students at the other school

Priests Publicly Support Schools

The priests of the parish need to publicly support each school within their parish.

Their homilies or other addresses and the support shown for each school at that school, at the other schools and at the parish, are very important

Principal Intervention for non-supportive staff and parents

Principals will also need to be aware of any lack of support of some staff and parents towards the other school/s.

Intervention may be necessary to allay the challenges and to show support for the other school/s.

Feeder School Visitations

Introduction

> Most secondary school staff appreciates visiting their primary feeder schools to speak with their students with the assistance of a professionally produced presentation.
>
> This helps students in the primary / elementary schools decide on the parish secondary school for higher school education.

The Visitation needs to be professionally produced and presented.

Role of Priests

The Parish Priest, or one of the local priests, should be a visible presence at these visitations.

Minimal presence could be as a vocal supporter of the schools at the beginning or end of the presentation.

A more in-depth presentation would have a far greater impact on the students and staff present.

This could take the form of a short PowerPoint of maximum 5 minutes placing the schools in the context of the parish and emphasizing how we are all working together as the People of God. The schools could assist or create this PowerPoint with, or for, the priests.

As this is usually a once a year presentation to a few class groups, the Priests would be strongly encouraged to place the date/s in their calendars, due to what should be considered its high importance.

Role of School Staff

The presence and support of key personnel from both the secondary and elementary / primary schools are essential.

- The Principal of the elementary / primary school introducing their guests holds considerable weight for the students and staff present, and likewise to the student's parents when informed of the day when at home soon afterwards.

- The elementary / primary class teachers hold much influence with their classes also. How they approach the presentation before and after will have a significant impact on their students. Supporting the secondary school is essential.

- (Any personal or professional challenges these teachers may have with the secondary school need to be dealt with in other forums. These unsupportive views must not be seen by their classes. In fact, outward support is necessary.)

- The Principal of the secondary school needs to be seen as the leader by the primary students and staff. Hence, the Principal's input is essential. If the Principal is unavailable then the most senior leadership team member should replace the Principal. In a general sense the more senior the school representative the more impact can be made.

- Other key secondary personnel could include: School Marketing Manager (SMM) acting as Master of Ceremonies (MC), Head of Middle School (HMS) and key student leaders from Years 8 and 12. The student leaders would best include past students of the particular elementary / primary school being visited and / or significant personalities e.g. College Captain, outstanding sports person or performing arts student, or other well known non-elected leader from that primary school.

- Five speakers is a good number depending on the type of presentation. Too few or too many speakers will often lose effectiveness.

Year Levels Visited

The last, second last and third last years of primary / elementary school are probably the best years with which to begin the presentation. However, this will depend on the state and country. (Many families seem to decide within the second or third last years which secondary school to send their child.)

Presentations would generally be given to each student in Years 4-6 or 5-7 depending on the state and country. The presentation to the higher year levels would be to support the one they received in the younger grade.

Each following year's presentation, for the higher year levels who received the presentation in a younger grade, needs to have differences yet maintain the core messages of the previous year.

Variety is needed for the students, but also support of the key messages for each year of the presentation. The variation could be in the form of:

- yearly updated College DVD and PowerPoints
- updated Prospectus
- different student speakers

Presentation Overview

Visitations are usually conducted in the few weeks before the school's (or Parish) Open Day.

Visitations are best done in the morning when everyone is feeling fresh.

Presentations are usually done for individual year levels. However, combinations may occur due to the primary school's needs.

Numbers of students attending each presentation should be appropriate. Too many students in one room at a time can easily limit the effectiveness of the morning. 80-100 students should be the maximum in a good sized room. Large auditoriums often do not suit these forms of engagement.

The whole presentation should be for about an hour or less.

The length would depend on the variety of resources brought from the secondary school.

Too much talk from teachers / administrators without visual aid will usually gain a negative impact.

Primary students particularly enjoy the visual presentations, the secondary students' addresses and the Principal's presentation (if succinct).

Room and Facilities

The room needs to be appropriate for the numbers of students present. Not too big or small. Good ventilation and lighting.

Facilities for data projection are also required.

It is also essential to bring a computer technician or other staff member to set up and be available for any break-down moments.

Use the primary school's data projection facilities, if appropriate. This is a good PR move also.

The computer technician needs to arrive earlier to evaluate the equipment and decide on the best approach.

All data projection facilities also need to be brought by the school as a back-up in case there is a failure at the primary school. (This does happen!)

It is not a good PR moment when there is equipment failure. However, be cool, attend to the problem and adjust the agenda to suit.

If at all possible, return to the data projection when the problem is solved. The computer expertise of the secondary school needs to be seen.

Preparation Before Visitations

- **Preparation for the Visitations requires school secretaries:**

  - Obtaining the numbers of each year level from each school to be visited

  - Counting of the required number of Prospectus and 'goodies / gifts' for each year level for each school and placing these in marked boxes. This would also require placing all inclusions in each prospectus

  - Arranging times and dates with each school for each year level and approximate arrival times of staff and students. (Computer technician arrives about 30 - 45 minutes before the others.)

  - Coordinating these times and dates with staff attending + advising staff of meeting times and places on the day

  - Letters for parents of each student attending from the secondary school advising of the event, date and times, and transport in teachers' cars is written and left with the Principal.

- **Preparation before the day also requires:**

  - Principal, Head of Middle School and SMM usually are the people to decide on the best students to attend each school

  - Principal invites these students to attend and to prepare an address

  - Permission letters are given to the students

  - Students advised usually by the Principal of the honor of being invited, expectations when away from the College, along with uniform, hair, jewellery expectations, etc

  - The students' addresses most often are coordinated by the HMS to avoid overlapping of ideas

  - Principal may like to hear each address prior. This allows for both support for each student from the highest office in the school (hence showing the importance of such event) plus a final check of what will be said.

Preparation on the day of the Visitation:

- HMS checks after roll call that students are at school. If not, HMS along with the Principal, make any necessary changes

- HMS reminds students of meeting times at the Office and uniform check is done

- Secretary places boxes of Prospectus and 'goodies / gifts' out for taking

- Computer Technician finalizes equipment including:

  * data projector
  * laptop with DVD and PowerPoint presentation already installed
  * necessary leads, power boards and computer cables etc
  * large screen.

- Computer technician departs allowing for an arrival of about 30-45 minutes prior to beginning of the first presentation.

- Other staff and students leave allowing for an arrival time of about 15 minutes before the presentation.

- All staff sign-in at the primary school's office on arrival and usually go with the Primary Principal to the venue. (Computer technician may often be taken / directed by a secretary.)

Sample Visitation Presentation Agenda

A possible Visitation Presentation agenda could be:

(All speakers must remember that Brevity is paramount!)

1. MC introduces the morning (advises that questions will be invited at end of morning, depending on time available)

2. Parish Priest welcomes everyone through prayer, says a few brief words of support for the schools and where possible shows a short 5 minute max PowerPoint linking the schools to the Parish

3. School's DVD is shown

4. PowerPoint - photos summarizing the previous year. Up to 180 photos could be shown. The MC gives a short explanation of each pic or group of pics. 3-5 second transitions from pic to pic.

5. Head of Middle School offers a few short comments and introduces the Student speakers

6. MC introduces the Principal. Principal gives a short address and distributes the College's Prospectus and talks through it. S/he invites students to the College's Open Day

7. Questions from students

8. On completion of the visit a sincere thanks to the elementary / primary Principal and teachers should be offered.

This is a wonderful opportunity for both the primary and secondary schools to further build on their partnerships.

Taster Days

Elementary / Primary students visiting their secondary school should lead to much shared joy, motivation and reputation building.

Overview

Planned days for students in the last two to three years of primary / junior school (and last year for reinforcement, if desired) from each of a secondary school's feeder schools, allows the students to experience life in a secondary school.

Having too many visiting students at any one time can be detrimental and may cause disruption to normal secondary classes. Both primary and secondary teachers and students would more than likely feel pressurized and not fully enjoy the experience.

Priest and Pastoral Associates Involvement

Once again it is important for the Priests and / or Pastoral Associates to be seen at these unique opportunities.

There may be a place for a beginning prayer and welcome of the primary / junior students to the secondary school for the day.

Otherwise just being around at different times throughout the day and having a chat with the students as they do various class activities or around the playground during lunch is immeasurable.

Different Experiences

Students experiencing different subjects to primary / elementary school, or different aspects of their regular subjects, should be the intention of each day.

Some of these areas could include: Graphics, Hospitality, Industrial Skills, Drama, Music / Band, Math or English through the use of IT, Advanced IT, etc.

Other physical aspects of the College could be highlighted through different activities e.g. the new gymnasium or pool, theatre, individual music rooms, workshops, data projection rooms, sacred space, etc.

Different schools visiting on different days are often easier to organize.

Day Plan

- The plan could be to have the visiting students are divided into different sized groups depending on the activities offered.

- The students would then rotate through a number of the activities over the course of the day.

- Having some of the secondary students in attendance to help and be involved is an often successful approach.

- A shared lunch with the Year 7/8 students (lowest secondary level) e.g. bar-b-q and drink is appreciated by all.

Teachers

Teachers need to be interested in, and prepared for, the event, for there to be a successful outcome.

Promotion of the Taster Days needs to be an integral part of the staff formation for a better appreciation of the School Marketing Plan (SMP).

Teachers taking each activity should be well prepared and be able to offer the best experience they can in their particular subject area.

The visiting elementary / primary teachers must feel genuinely welcomed and an integral part of the Taster Day.

Transport

The biggest expense would be the cost of buses for schools not close by. This is best paid for by the secondary school (a good PR opportunity), unless other arrangements have been made.

Parish Recognition Night
or...

A once a year event for showcasing the outstanding generosity of parishioners, staff and students to the life of the parish.

Overview

This may be a viable and rewarding experience for a number of volunteers and staff.

It may also not be a possibility due to the modest nature of most volunteers.

Each Parish would need to consider this on its local merits.

Many parishes would benefit from this as a form of marketing as it encourages certain types of people to get involved in parish life. In general even the most modest inwardly appreciate sincere thanks.

This may take the form of a dinner, lunch or breakfast, and include a Recognition Certificates presentation.

It should include some form of entertainment such as an after-dinner speaker, comedian and a PowerPoint / DVD presentation of the Parish's yearly highlights. The speaker or comedian may even be a parishioner.

Other Options

Thank-You Dinner / Lunch / Breakfast

Some parishes may choose to have a Thank-You Dinner / Lunch / Breakfast instead.

This is a social get together for all the volunteers. Most people would thoroughly enjoy this experience.

A special after-meal speaker / comedian and PowerPoint would add considerably to the event.

Church Marketing Resources + Instructions

Church Marketing Resources + Instructions

First impressions very much count!

Two critical areas necessary as first points of contact are based around the initial contact with the parish, as well as the basic resources used in all marketing campaigns.

When prospective parishioners, school enrolments and others in the community see or hear someone or some visual / audio associated with the parish an impression is made. Make it a good one!

Often you have very little time to make an impact!

Images and people associated with the 'front' of the church or parish are critical. From the greeting received at church, to the phone answering style and stationery used, nothing should be left to chance.

Just as important are the images, voices and sounds used in your marketing! Spend considerable time preparing for, selecting and presenting these resources.

Photos, DVDs and CDs speak a thousand words! As do the voices used in any production or conversation with the parish.

Headings

Marketing Resources – What Should be Used?
Parish Information Kit
Producing a Parish Information Kit
Photos
Parish DVD / CD
Parish Staff and Greeters
Telephone and TXTing
Telephone On-Hold
Newsletter

Commercially Produced Newsletter
Flyers
Posters
Brochures
Signs and Signboards
Promotional Items
Yearbook

Marketing Resources - What Should be Used?

Overview

Each resource could be successful depending upon:

quality and quantity of the production
expertise of the CMM
willingness of the CMM to explore possibilities
use of associated staff
having a suitable budget available.

Considerable Range of Resource Options

The target audience will also impact on what is best to use, and how best to produce and present these resources to the audience. Various surveys of the target audience, and of those associated with this group e.g. parishioners and staff, will assist with this information.

Discussions with other nearby parishes and schools, along with the diocesan personnel, will also be of a significant assistance in choosing the appropriate marketing resources.

Examples Used in this Book

Below is a list of the most commonly used marketing resources for parishes. These are explored throughout this e-book:

- Key Stakeholders
- Website
- Media
- Parish and School Staff
- Parish Information Kit
- DVD / CD / Videos
- e/i-Newsletters, Glossy Newsletter and Parish Newsletter
- e/i-Brochures / Brochures
- e/i-Flyers / Flyers

- Photos, Photos, Photos
- Telephone & TXTing
- Telephone On-Hold
- Email
- Signs and Signboards
- Information Evenings
- Parish Magazine or 'Yearbook'
- Posters
- 'Staged' Events
- Parish Open Day
- Taster Days
- Parish Recognition Night / Parish Dinner
- Promotional Items
- Advertising in newspapers and magazines, and on radio and television

Parish Information Kit

> The first document most prospective parishioners need presented to them is the Parish Information Kit.
>
> This helps enormously with the Welcoming Process.

Introduction

> **It is best to also have this Kit also on the parish and school websites in an easily downloadable pdf format.**

You will need to decide on the number of Kits you need printed as hardcopies.

A good Kit should last three years. Some parishes like to change each couple of years, though.

(Other parishes like to keep the same material for many years. Could I suggest that this may send a wrong message – that the parish is stagnant and bereft of new ideas!)

Due to the usual amount of time and expense involved, three years is ideal.

The Kit's production is possibly best done early in the year. This allows for it to be used that year, along with a more relevant use of lasting photos.

Content

The Parish Marketing Kit markets key aspects of the parish e.g.:

- Welcoming + Introduction to Parish and details of the program

- Vision and Mission Statement

- Sacramental and Liturgical Life of the Parish

- Social Justice, Welfare and Pastoral Care Life of the Parish

- Social, Cultural and Sporting Life of the Parish

- Key roles / committees e.g.: Parish Priest, Priests, Pastoral Associate, Parish Manager, Parish Pastoral Council, Finance Committee

- Plant and locations of key facilities e.g. churches, schools, presbytery

- Special Offerings e.g.

    * Half-Way Houses

    * IT Hardware, Software and Support Program.

Invitation to be involved in the life of the parish, through:

prayer life,
voluntary work
financial support, etc.

Branding is integral to the appearance, look and feel of this document: Parish Branding Logo, colors and design layout are essential.

Inclusions

Various removable inclusions are an important aspect of any Kit. (See 'Parish Information Kit Production')

Photos

Photos are also integral to the presentation and need to be of a high quality in content and production.

People are initially usually attracted to the photos and then move to the text.

Good photos throughout encourage the exploration of the all important text on each particular page.

Photos on each page should:

- appear natural, not with a photographic studio or specially lit appearance

- be unique to that page's theme (an unrelated photo detracts from the page)

- have content which highlights a particular aspect of the theme

- normally have happy, well presented people of varying ages – cover all from infants to the elderly, but suited to the particular theme on that page

- include background photos on some pages which support the theme

- be cropped to necessary parameters to highlight the aspect.

Outside photographers should be sourced if the school's equipment, photographers or creative skills are not of this standard.

Producing a Parish Information Kit

Most good printing firms will have professional graphic artists on staff, or acting as consultants. These people will do as much as is required by the CMM on the overall publication, before it is printed.

Commercial Printers and Graphic Artists

You may do everything on your own software in the parish or at the school and give the printer firm your final copy in a suitable format, e.g. pdf.

This is quite acceptable and will save financially, but often doesn't allow for another professional opinion.

However, an opinion could be sort after you completing your creation first and then sending it, sometimes at an extra cost.

Your printer's graphic artist is often a good source for creative ideas regarding the layout, page colors, page backgrounds, photo placement, text section lengths and text fonts, etc.

A good balanced approach is to use ideas from both the parish and graphic artist.

Production Plan and Tips

The CMM would:

- request quotes from three or more printing firms and request the type of support you would receive e.g. graphic artist

- Be clear about your requirements:
  - number of color and grayscale pages
  - possible number of photos per page
  - quality and type of paper

- ⋆ quality of outside cardboard or thick paper shell
  - ⋆ insert sleeve
  - ⋆ any tear-out sections etc.

- do initial mock-up designs of each page on either sketch paper or computer software e.g. Microsoft Publisher, including placement of photos and text, background photos and colors, in accordance with your church's branded style e.g. swirls appropriately positioned ...

**... but not the same for each page, as this will become monotonous...
variety is needed.**

- write the text according to the predetermined themes in the required lengths - other key people could assist here e.g. Parish Priest, Priests, Pastoral Associate, Parish Manager, Finance Manager, Committee Leaders, School Principals, Aged Care Manager.

  - ⋆ Brevity is the key.

- select photo scenes, props and suitable people to highlight the text

- arrange for photo taking - take many photos, varying the scene angles and people positions and any props' positions.

- your yearly collection of photos may have some classics, which should be included - some fantastic photos may be a year or more old. These would include those one-off photos which couldn't be taken again. A few of these will not hurt.

- select the best photos for the layout

- gain second opinions of the text, selected pics and layout from the Parish Priest and other key people as decided in consultation with the Parish Priest

- proof text - good to have key literary people here e.g. Schools' Librarian, Head of English

- take the whole proposal to the graphic artist - this would include the mock-up page designs in either sketches or digital forms, along with the digital text in Rich Text Format and photos on a disc.

- allow the graphic artist to design each page according to your suggestions but allow them license to offer various other suggestions

- have each page emailed to you when completed and check it for layouts:

* proof it another time and gain second opinions
* make decisions and feed these decisions back to the graphic artist

---

- Best to make decisions before asking for adjustments - avoids time wasting.

- Sometimes you may ask for a couple of variation options to look at before making the final decision. This is normally acceptable, however it shouldn't be the norm as the quote doesn't usually allow for many changes to the printer's completed pages. Most printing firms are quite good though, especially for good clients!

- have all adjusted pages sent to you for final inspection and proofing

- put together as if a complete Parish Information Kit, and go through it with the Parish Priest and any other key people as if you were prospective parishioners

- advise printer of final changes

- proof these final changes

- the CMM signs-off on the finished product

- wait one to two weeks for printing to be complete - often a good idea to get a printing timeline commitment from the printers.

Inserts

A good Parish Information Kit would often have an insert sleeve for inclusions. This sleeve could also be used for other purposes e.g. if an envelope size, it could be a tear off card, with free post registration to the parish on the front and a back which encourages prospective parishioners to send the 'card' back requesting further information or a meeting. This allows for personal contact to be made.

Some inclusions could be the parish brochures e.g.:

- Parish Staff and Specialist Support Staff – roles, general policies and offerings

- Sacramental Programs - details and personnel

- Social Justice, Welfare and Pastoral Care Programs and personnel

- Family support structures and programs

- Parish Pastoral Council - personnel including short biographies and role of Council

- Welcoming – general overview for new parishioners

- Deanery overview – supplied by deanery with each parish's input

- Parish DVD is a major inclusion. (*If the DVD is produced at and by the parish's or school's personnel, then this not only emphasizes the major points on the DVD but also shows an important aspect of the parish's or school's IT status, along with the skills of both staff, parishioners or students.*)

These inclusions should be on either standard stationery or adjusted design paper, which still maintains the general branding style.

The pages need to each appeal individually i.e. if each was on parish stationery a sameness would be apparent.

Changes of design for these inclusions should include:

- the logo in possible varying sizes and positions

- normal regularly used graphic designs maybe partially used e.g. if there are swirls / lines normally at both the top and bottom of each page of stationery, you may just use one of these designs on certain pages

- the use of folded A3 pages is often quite effective for variety.

Take time to plan and implement.

No short cuts.

Photos

Photos! Photos! Photos!

"A picture tells a thousand words"

CRITICAL FOR SUCCESS!

Introduction

Never has this saying been truer than when it comes to marketing the parish.

The enjoyable moments, the Baptisms and Confirmations, the successes, the socializing, the friendships, the games, the sport and the arts, the venue / church, the events, etc are recorded for perpetuity.

The photos will be used in so many ways throughout the year.

These will also be a part of recorded history.

All the forms of marketing will use selections of these photos.

Sometimes videos or DVDs / CDs may be needed as well.

If this is done properly, there will more than likely be hundreds, if not, thousands of photos taken each year.

How to Take Good Photographs – Website Examples

These days there are many suggestions to be found on the internet about how to take good photographs. A few suggestions, from when this chapter was written, would include at Kodak, BBC and Basic-Digital-Photography.com .

Doing a search of your search engine using a phrase such as 'taking good digital photos' achieves a vast variety of options.

Photos onto Church Website

A good selection of these should be placed on the parish's website's Gallery soon after the being taken. This allows for positive discussion from the parishioners, as well as being available for the whole community.

Most people thoroughly enjoy seeing photos of themselves, their peers and friends while at an enjoyable event or achieving something special.

The Church Marketing Manager (CMM) should usually be responsible for what photos are placed on the website so that these are appropriate and show images in line with the CMP.

It is often a good practice to have the Parish Manager, IT coordinator, or system's administrator, as a final back up editor just prior to them placing the pictures onto the webpage.

Church Photographers

Taking and selecting thousands of photos per year should not be daunting.

The reasons for this will become evident once the right photographic personnel are involved and the culture of photographing most happenings is formed.

The parish would be served best by having a specific person as their main photographer, along with back-up photographers for big events or for when the main photographer is not present. These people would hopefully be parishioners or staff members so as to have an insider's appreciation of how the parish operates and to save on costs.

These people may include the CMM, however it is often best that the CMM be a support photographer and be someone who is available at most times for those unexpected photos. Often photographs are needed while the CMM is arranging various other happenings simultaneously.

The main photographers need a good working knowledge of photography and the camera/s they will use.

> **For those special occasions not any photo will do. The setting, lighting, people in the photo and best pose, etc are critical.**

Sometimes an outside professional photographer may be needed.

However, having staff members or parishioners professionally trained is a viable option. The people chosen should have experience either personally or professionally from within or outside the school environment.

> **Taking the correct promotional photo is an art.**
> **Do not skimp on this as the impact on the marketing campaign**
> **will be adversely affected.**

Digital Cameras

Digital cameras are now the norm with Digital SLR cameras being the best. However, most good 6+MB digital cameras could be used for most events. There is so much information available on the internet these days. I would suggest using your web search engine and phrases such as 'digital cameras best buys' and digital camera reviews' to access some very good information. A good review site I find is at Choice.

The DSLR camera should be used for special photos from main events or for photos with a special promotional use e.g. parish magazines, flyers and advertisements.

Digital cameras allow for many more photos than once were normally taken with film cameras. This often allows for a better quality of photo to be selected. The more photos to choose from invariably allows for at least one or more to stand out in quality and relevance.

It also allows for quick selection and usage of selected pics, as well as immediate deletion.

Virtually all the photos taken will not be made into prints. This will gain considerable financial savings for the parish. Also, the digital cameras are relatively inexpensive, including the necessary DSLR ones.

Film cameras are a challenge

Using film cameras can cause many difficulties, the first being the availability of the film itself. Next will be finding a photographic laboratory to develop and print these. Then there is the issue of cost.

Having finally obtained the prints these will need to be scanned or supplied on CD for most of the uses envisaged.

This could take considerable time, which in reality is a major waste of time and money.

Digital cameras allow you to see instantly if your photos are successful and what changes you need to make.

Parish DVD / CD

The parish DVD / CD says much about the parish and is often seen as 'cool'!

Introduction

The Parish DVD / CD need to be professionally produced. It is preferable to be produced in-house at your parish or local school for marketing, professional and educational reasons.

Whether to use a DVD or CD depends on file size of the final production. A CD is used to about 700MB and a DVD to about 4.7GB.

To be able to promote this in-house aspect using parish or school IT expertise and equipment, and staff and students is especially good.

Purpose

The DVD / CD content emphasize the Parish's:

- staff and students' IT skills (who produced the DVD)

- parish or school's IT resources (which were used to create the DVD)

- spiritual, welfare, pastoral, sporting, artistic and cultural offerings

- facilities

- staff and students through its content and production.

Production

Many parishes and schools now have personnel who will be able to do this. Various software courses from technical colleges, universities, school systems and commercial businesses are available for interested staff.

This whole production is a **time consuming process**.

Outsourced Costs: If this needs to be outsourced commercially, be prepared for quite a large budgetary challenge.

Even outsourcing sections e.g. videoing, will be **relatively expensive**.
Production Process

Production Plan

The DVD / CD production should best have:

- a plan developed by the Producer, usually the Church Marketing Manager (CMM)

- the Producer needs to take a real hands-on approach, including Directing (or overseeing this), the videoing and overseeing music, graphics, backgrounds and editing

- a general outline of scenes, order and videoing dates and times

- leading questions for those being interviewed (preferably parishioners, Parish Priest or other key people such as another priest or Pastoral Associate and sometimes staff, and given to them well in advance of taping, and discussed with them prior to recording)

- videoing done by a person with considerable competence (this may need to be outsourced if staff aren't qualified or proficient enough for this)

- graphics, especially for opening and closing scenes, interviewee names and key points being highlighted throughout as subtexts or overlays

- graphic style should be based on the parish's branding e.g. as used for stationery

- background music, preferably written and performed by parishioners, students or staff

- a text for any overdubbing needed to complete any deficient but necessary scenes or for greater emphasis of certain aspects

- a good production length is often between 7 and 10 minutes when complete.

Videoing Skills

The camera operator will need to know:

- the camera's functions intimately
- the use of dolly rails, for moving the camera in a line while videoing
- about lighting, especially the use of natural and artificial sources, angles etc

- sound, including boom, desk and lapel microphones
- the use of blue screens, which allow varied background scenes being added.

When videoing is complete, special expertise is needed for each of the following processes.

Video Editing Software Examples

There are numerous video editing software options available at rates beginning around $US30 and going quite high.

Some video editing software examples are:

Adobe Premiere Elements 8 is a popular simple program and usually available for <$US80. See details at http://www.adobe.com/products/premiereel/

Adobe Premier Pro CS4 is a professional level program available for over $US750. See details at http://www.adobe.com/products/premiere/

iMovie for Apple users is the basic version and is part of the iShop suite available for usually <$US80.
See details at http://store.apple.com/us/product/MB966Z/A/iLife-09?fnode=MTY1NDAzOA&mco=MTM3NDc5MjU

Final Cut Studio for Apple users is the professional version priced over $US950.
See details at http://store.apple.com/us/product/MB642Z/A?fnode=MTY1NDAzOA&mco=MTA4MjgwNzk

Final Cut Express 4.0 for Apple users is a smaller version for just under $US200
See details at http://store.apple.com/us/product/MB278Z/A?fnode=MTY1NDAzOA&mco=MTA4MjgwODY

PowerDirector 8 by Cyberlink is a popular inexpensive software and usually available for <$US100.
See details at: http://www.cyberlink.com/products/powerdirector/overview

VideoStudio Pro X2 by Corel is a popular inexpensive software and usually available for <$US60.
See details at http://www.corel.com/servlet/Satellite/us/en/Product/1175714228541#tabview=tab0

Advice for Hardware and Software Purchases

As the market is continually changing, and when necessary there is the need to purchase the best cost effective equipment and software, CMMs should regularly speak to:

- Churches and schools which have recently produced good video recordings
- commercial stores
- commercial videographers
- other CMMs
- Diocesan Communications and Marketing Manager
- IT staff at parish and school
- explore various hardware / video editing software reviews on the internet.

Post Videoing Sequences

The selection of best video sequences is time consuming. At least twice the length of the video / DVD taken, is needed to effectively make these selections.

(In general, a 1 hour recording will need at least 2 hours of viewing to enable a good quality sequence selections.)

- The video / DVD / 'Memory Stick' needs to be initially viewed fully with rough notes taken by the viewer on possible sequences to be used.

- Next it is viewed again with specific sequences selected and noted.

- Often another viewing of the already selected sequences is needed to make the final selection of sequences that will be used.

- Editing into the chosen format is then required. The selected scenes are imported into a relevant computer software program and arranged as required on the computer.

- Graphics, photos, sound and voiceovers, along with background music are then added.

Part of Church Marketing Plan

The produced DVD / CD would then become part of the Church Marketing Plan (CMP).

Finished product will be made onto DVDs or CDs for distribution. (There is a multicopier available for DVD / CD copying. This is a worthwhile purchase.)

DVDs / CDs are often:

- shown on a computer monitor positioned in the Parish's and School's Front Offices

- embedded on to the website or as 'You Tube' embedding (see embedding details at Video Uploads section in this e-book)

- available through the website e.g. by ordering via email, telephone (or Online Shop, if this is an aspect of the website)

- sent to prospective parishioners on request through Parish's or School's Offices

- shown to prospective parishioners, students and parents at Parish Open Days, Visitations to Schools or on School Taster Days of prospective enrolments

- shown as a loop in a strategic position at Feast Days, Parish and School Open Days and Information Nights, etc.

- also used for
    * Liturgy and Prayer
    * Feast Day / Open Day presentations
    * Adult Education sessions
    * Youth activities
    * Schools' Graduations
    * Schools' Awards Night / Night of Excellence
    * Record of parish events throughout the year

Internal Promotion

Parishioners, school staff, students and parents should be made aware of this production.

All should have the opportunity of viewing it.

This is a great help in building support from these groups as they see another aspect of the parish and school in action, a cutting-edge one at that. Many people enjoy talking about what they saw on DVD / CD.

Church Staff and Greeters

The first person a new parishioner meets may be the Greeter at the front of the church, or one who knocks on their front door to welcome them to the parish.

The first face to face contact with the staff is usually through the Parish Office.

Introduction

The Parish Office needs to depict the church's vision and mission philosophy.

This is initially done through its physical appearance and the attitude of the staff present at the Front Desk (and other staff visible from the front counter).

The volunteers who greet people need to be well versed in this skill and fully informed as to what the parish has to offer.

Nothing beats a genuine smile and open welcome.

As with all marketing, it is the first impression which counts considerably to the overall perception of the visitor / guest / new parishioner / commercial representative, etc.

The Parish Office should be visibly welcoming, as should the Front Desk staff.

A professional appearance of both office and staff is critical.

Branding

Wherever possible, the parish's branding should be apparent, for example:

- parish internal colors (not necessarily parish colors or outside paint branded colors)

- a branded poster of the Vision and Mission Statement

- general office layout, wall hangings and features (well designed and not cluttered)

- office staff in uniforms.

A lack of branding uniformity sends the wrong message.

The perception it creates in the visitor varies. It may express a lack of organization or leadership.

It may say there are financial difficulties within the parish or school.

To avoid any negative perception is very important.

Front Desk Monitor

A good feature would be to include a computer monitor attached to a computer or DVD player which plays looped DVDs produced by or for the parish. The parish and school DVDs / CDs are often the best general productions to feature.

However, special features based on specific themes produced throughout the year have a unique place, for example the upcoming Feast or Open Days or special sacramental day or event.

Productions shown could also include PowerPoints of selected photos, which tell a particular story, for example:

- a summary of key events and happenings for that particular Church season or year just gone

- highlights of the recent Parish Dinner or Musical

- special youth activities / groups / liturgies

- the latest purchase of key resources, e.g. new facilities, etc.

- social justice and welfare involvement

- age care visitations by school children

Telephone & TXTing

The telephone is still a primary form of communication for the church.

There is becoming a more opportune time to use TXTing for mobile phones through computer or cell / mobile dispatches.

Most people still enjoy actually hearing someone's voice when communicating. This personalizes the conversation. It often replaces the face-to-face contact / interview.

Parish Office Response to Calls

The telephone greeting is extremely important. This may be the first moment of verbal contact and sets the tone for the conversation. Politeness and genuine feelings of assistance need to be espoused. The Parish Office introduction needs to include:

- a greeting
- the church or parish name
- who is speaking and
- offer of assistance.

For example, "Good morning … this is Leanne from St Mary's Parish Coomera …how may I help you / direct your call…?"

This person should have the skills to ascertain who would best deal with the caller. For many, if not most calls, the receptionist would be able to meet the needs of the caller.

Otherwise, this would often be by noting the reason for the call and transferring the call to the relevant person's line if s/he has a line.

The call should not normally be sent directly through to the staff member without first advising that staff member who is on the line.

If the transfer was not possible, it would require taking a note of a callback number, name and short reason for the return call. This would then be passed to the staff member usually via email or telephone note placed in the appropriate location e.g. staff pigeon hole, call tray, etc.

Staff Voicemails

Key staff should have a voicemail service. Each staff member with a voicemail should include the following in his / her recording:

- a greeting
- who is speaking
- the person's role
- parish name
- offer of assistance
- request for details.

For example, "Hello, you have reached the phone of Sally Fielding, Parish Secretary at St Mary's Parish, Coomera. As I am unavailable at the moment, please leave a short message and telephone number (after the beep) and I will return your call as soon as possible..."

Challenging Calls

The Parish Office receptionist should have skills to deal with the irate caller:

- calmness and empathy are the best tools
- acknowledge to the caller that s/he has a genuine concern
- advise that you will do whatever is necessary and possible to solve the difficulty
- pass on to the relevant person if available.

Otherwise if the person required, or someone else who could deal with the call more effectively than the receptionist, is not available, then it is best to:

- listen
- empathise
- take notes
- advise the person needing to be contacted will return the call ASAP.

The receptionist may also need to:

- just be a sounding board
- remain calm and empathetic
- genuinely sounding to offer the best advice for the solution, if appropriate.

A 'thick skin' is also sometimes a prerequisite, as well as an appreciation that the call is not to be taken personally.

Staff Response to the Challenging Call

The staff member who receives the transferred call also needs the above skills.

The telephonist needs to advise the receiving staff member of the nature of the call.

A major fear of staff is the irate caller or the call needing to be made to an irate parishioner.

Fortunately, experience is a wonderful thing. Once a staff member has dealt successfully with this type of call and the whole process a few times, it becomes much simpler, if not quite rewarding to handle the issue as a 'challenge'.

Remember, listen and hear, empathise, offer solution/s if appropriate, follow-up as needed.

It is often a good idea to treat all difficulties as challenges and not problems. Hence, challenging oneself to find a solution.

Like any challenge it is good to practise various scenarios. Staff should spend time **role playing** these types of calls (and interviews), and being evaluated and assisted by those who have the skills. This is a learning experience and not a 'test'. Those with the skills should be willing to lead these practice sessions.

TXTing and Church Marketing

This is a new field for most people. However, due to the enormous use of cell / mobile phone by so many of our parishioners, it is now time to consider communicating to our parishioners via txting.

Interested parishioners would be invited to leave their mobile numbers with the parish office. The secretary would txt the parishioners as needed. This might be for an invitation to a meeting or group activity or an adjusted time for a religious ceremony. The reasons for using txting are only limited by the normal number of reasons to communicate with our parishioners.

The txt messages may be delivered directly from the mobile / cell phone for individuals or smaller groups and via the computer for large groups.

For more information check the options in your particular country. Some examples may be found at: <u>White Pages</u> in USA, <u>Nokia</u> in Europe and <u>Telstra</u> in Australia.

Telephone On-Hold

> The Telephone On-Hold message is a unique way to market the church to a 'captive listener'.

Introduction

The On-Hold message should play whenever:

- a call is being transferred to an internal line

- when the caller is placed on hold while the receptionist is waiting for a response from a staff member i.e. checking if the staff member will take the call immediately or return the call

- when the telephonist is gaining information for the caller.

Production

The message should be one recorded by, or for, the parish.

Playing the radio or general music is a lost opportunity.

Using one or more radio advertisements recorded for the parish is one such method.

Always seek written permission from the copyright owners if the parish doesn't own the copyright.

This method comes across as very professional and informative. It is usually an advertisement with general content produced in an exciting format with appealing background music. (However, specific advertisements are also produced for radio and might not suit this on-hold purpose.)

With computer software that most parishes and schools now have, quite professional quality advertisements can be the norm.

Involving the parish school is a good proposition for parish / school relationships and effective for keeping the cost for production minimal.

A reasonable approach to the school is necessary.

Parishes can't always expect the schools to produce everything they need or according to the parish's timeline. Costs should also be met by the parish.

**Sometimes schools cannot meet the parish's expectation
e.g. due to time restrictions, curriculum or quality of product needed.**

Planned Recordings

Parish / School production allows for specific content to be easily used for a specific audience at a specific time of the year.

The CMM should normally have the year segmented into themes for On Hold messages e.g.: often based on the liturgical year and other key parish events.

---

*The On-Hold message often invites telephone callers to the church and
an invitation to explore the church's website, where possible.*

Script

With On Hold messages the script needs to be as succinct as radio adverts. The difficulty is the brevity required.

Key words and phrases need to pepper the sentences used.

Looped Play of Recording

The On Hold message should be a looped message of about 30-45 seconds in length. Rarely would someone on-hold be on longer than this.

If these are on longer, then a repeat of the message will emphasize it to the caller.

Newsletter

The Church Newsletter is often the parish's best regular form of information giving to parishioners.

Regular Weekly Publication

Regular weekly publication is needed for best success.

The readership should often be expanded to schools and other interested parishes and even to other willing sources e.g. parent and school businesses for display in reception rooms, offices etc.

Website Updates

The parish's website needs to be updated weekly, with each newsletter uploaded to it.

A collection of the year's newsletters on the website is appreciated by many parishioners and others wanting to get an overview of the year's progress.

Professional Presentation

A professional publication is needed.

The parish's branding is very important and needs to be strategically positioned throughout the pages.

Photos 'tell a thousand words' and whenever possible should be used. Always include captions including details about the photo and the names of people from left to right.

Appropriate content, quality and sizing are essential for success.

Many parishes use an A3 'shell' which is professionally and commercially printed and is branded accordingly. The parish's photocopiers add the weekly detail to the 'shell'.

Inserts, usually of A4 size or smaller, are added for any additional information.

Effectiveness of Content

It can be argued that most people read only the front page, which is usually written by the Parish Priest. If this is the case then the most important detail needs to be included here.

It follows that the newsletter's length be appropriate so that time and money is not wasted.

A good coverage of recent and upcoming events and activities is the primary purpose of the newsletter.

Some form of weekly rotation of topics / staff or parishioners presenting articles may be needed for effectiveness.

Staff and parishioner leaders should be encouraged to participate but according to certain parameters, especially length.

Brevity

Brevity is once again paramount to these stories.

This is often difficult for many people. These people need to be educated as to the best means of getting their information read in the newsletter.

Most importantly, staff and parishioner leaders need to feel valued for their input to the newsletter.

Sponsorship Dilemma

Many argue that to minimize costs, the last page, or other sections within the newsletter, should be given over to sponsorship, preferably from the businesses of parishioners.

Others would say that if sponsorship isn't needed then a clean uninhibited newsletter can be produced. This is so that the parish isn't seen as a commercial enterprise but as a stand-alone religious institute.

Many would also argue that advertisements aren't usually read.

When advertising is included in the newsletter, parishes need to be in philosophical alignment with the advertising company's principles of advertising and the particular adverts used.

If the parish can negotiate their own suppliers as advertisers, this should result in better success for the parish, due to the often localized nature of the adverts i.e. supporting the local community and all the goodwill this generates.

Advertisements need to be carefully selected so as to not impose on the overall production. The main purpose of the newsletter is not to advertise certain products.

The decision often comes down to the parish's budget restraints.

Layout Development

Parishes may have one or two staff who receive and do the newsletter's layout. This is good organizational practice.

If staff and parishioner leaders can electronically send their stories this improves the time taken and in a number of ways the effectiveness of the presentation. Electronic methods would be through the parish's computer networks or as an email attachment.

This method should be considered essential for economy of time and expense reasons.

The attachments should include photos, photo captions and directions to where photos are stored on any network.

The Parish Priest, or designated staff member, would need to decide on specific articles for each week's publication. Some articles may need to be delayed in line with the rotation method of weekly article selection.

Proofing is essential!

Commercial Newsletter

A 12-16 page professionally produced and printed commercial newsletter could play a significant role as part of the CMP.

This should also be available on the website for viewing and as a pdf document for downloading.

Introduction

This is a significantly different form of the newsletter, which has a wider distribution field, contains a large number of photos and stories written by key people within the parish, and is produced at a key, or key times, within the church and parish year.

It would be commercially printed in whatever format, paper type, etc felt best for each church.

Frequency

Due to its specialty, one or more of these publications could be done yearly. The decision would often be based on the budget, and availability of suitable content and photos.

The newsletter would highlight various aspects of the parish's and schools' lives up to the publication date/s and promote upcoming church and school events.

There are a number of suitable times of the year for publication, such as:

- Before Holy Week and / or Advent Christmas to prepare and promote the upcoming season and celebrations

- After Holy Week and / or Advent Christmas to promote what the parish and schools did during this time. This could encourage more parish involvement when people see what the parish does.

- Before or After a special sacramental celebration, especially if a significant person is in celebrating or in attendance e.g. Bishop

- End of Term 1 / Semester 1 to link in with the school year

- Before or After the Parish's Feast Day or special Parish event

Distribution

The key distribution points could be:

- Churches and Parish Office
- Front of each parish church
- own or feeder Schools (to highlight upcoming or past events and achievements, keep school informed and further develop support for the parish from its school community)
- Neighboring Parishes
- Local commercial and professional enterprises, especially those owned, managed, etc by parishioners
- Deanery or Diocesan Expos / Fairs etc

Color or Grayscale

> Color pages are by far the best in appearance and hence are enticing to the reader.

Pages come in sets of four i.e. a 16 page A4 newsletter would have four A3 sized sheets of paper folded into A4 sized pages.

A good use of both color and grayscale would be: outside and inside sheets in color, others in grayscale i.e. pages 1, 2, 7, 8, 9, 10, 15, and 16 in color.

If you were only to use four pages of color to save on costs then the outside pages are best for this.

Layout and Content

> The success of the front page is critical. Most people will decide whether to read the newsletter based on how the front page makes them feel.

A catchy Banner Title is important e.g. AQUINAS.COMmunity

The layout needs to match the branding style.

It is necessary to have the major story as the lead story. A good picture is also essential.

This story needs to appeal to the great majority of readers. Some topics which invariably attract attention are to do with:

- New Parish Priest or Priest or Principal / Leadership Team member / Specialist

- New or successful welfare or social justice involvements

- Outstanding successes of sacramental programs

- Youth and Adult retreats / activities – what happens, when, who goes, benefits, etc

- Street Retreats for helping homeless and disadvantaged on the street

- 'Angels Kitchen' for helping homeless

- New sacramental programs or celebrations being developed and need for parishioner involvement

- Welcoming invitation to new parishioners to what the parish has to offer

- Adult or Children's educational programs

- Outstanding successes of parishioners or students at cultural, educational, sporting or welfare endeavors

- Major parish event such as the upcoming Parish Musical

- Building programs, including refurbishments

- Large expenditures / developmental programs e.g. buildings, computers

- Cutting-edge technological developments

- Major celebrations e.g. 50th year of parish or school: major combined schools liturgy

- Major upcoming or recently passed events, sacramental programs with a special angle which would appeal to a large cross-section of readers.

Having other key stories promoted on the **front page** is very helpful to the reader. This could occur through boxed-in key words or brief summaries of stories, or captioned photos, with page numbers directing to the stories inside.

Color is also essential and appealing.

The **back page** is similar to the front page yet with different emphasizes. Color, good stories, photos and lead-in phrases or photos are needed.

This is also often where parish details are displayed at the bottom of the page, often in a boxed section, for follow-up e.g. key people's roles and contact numbers, webaddress, parish address.

Promotional boxes also work well here e.g. upcoming Feast or Open Day basic details.

> **Photos** of a good quality are the key to a successful presentation.

Once again, if photos have been taken of every event since the start of the year, there should be enough detail for the newsletter.

> Full sized **parish** or **school advertisements** also work well in these publications.

This is another avenue to reproduce the flyer (see 'Flyers') for Open Day previously devised.

> **Photographic Collages** of events are also very effective.

The brushed edges of each photo is one effective method of combining these. When done on color pages these achieve considerable success.

Some events could be: Retreats and Reflection Days, Liturgies, other Sacraments, Youth Helping Youth Program, Street Retreats for Homeless, Angels Kitchen, Sport Days, Drama, Music, Art and Dance.

Production procedures

Production procedures are similar to those for a new Parish Information Kit (see inside this e-book; along with the School Prospectus (See 'Producing a Prospectus' in _School Marketing e-Handbook: Easy to Use Guide to Market Your School_).

Flyers

Flyers target the neighboring suburbs and schools en mass.

Flyers have been found to be a very successful marketing form.

Introduction

The best approach is to have a specific theme on the flyer, which needs to be apparent e.g. Holy Week, Advent / Christmas, Social Justice Programs, Youth Events or Aged Care Developments, etc.

Having a general themed flyer to promote the church will often say to the reader that the church needs more people. Many people react against this.

Purpose

The purpose is to inform the surrounding suburbs and potential families within the parish of the advantages of your parish to the community.

This should develop a positive discussion over time.

The prestige should be raised or confirmed. Interest should be increased with potential new families to your church and parish.

Target Group

You only need to target potential parishioners' suburbs within the parish.

Cost

As a general guide at time of printing, you will need to allow around six thousand dollars to print and distribute around 60 000 flyers.

Your own production costs prior to printing are on top of this.

Layout

It is best for cost efficiency to use both side.

One side would be devoted to the main theme e.g. Holy Week.

The other side espouses those points you want marketed and formatted in a clear, appealing way. Some suggestions would be:

- Welcoming Program
- Sacramental Programs
- Social Justice Programs
- Family Programs.

More than four themes could become too busy and not appear interesting enough to explore.

> Quality photos, brief texts, color and branding are key aspects of any flyer.

Paper Type

Paper type is also important e.g. glossy or recycled buffed paper both attract attention but in different ways. Photocopier paper doesn't really suit this form of marketing, unless the budget is too stretched, or you have a very good quality print.

Some recycled paper is difficult to read properly.

Font style and size, along with colors used, need special attention on recycled paper.

(Remember your branding style and colors.)

Size of Flyer

Often the best sized flyer is a double sided A4.

A high quality production is necessary.

Flyers are best not folded for distribution to the churches, Parish Office and schools. This often allows for maximum impact – see the outstanding front page.

Flyers are folded for letterbox deliveries by the printers. These are usually folded in thirds along the long side to fit easily into the box.

Delivery Methods

1. Delivery of flyers to schools and professional and commercial enterprises is also another way of keeping contact with these key personnel - Parishioners, Principals, Office staff. The CMM is often in the best position to maintain or improve these relationships and hence do the deliveries.

2. A reputable letter box delivery service is engaged to deliver to the chosen suburbs. These are usually found in the Yellow Pages or similar advertising publications, on the web, or through reputation.

3. Your commercial printing business would usually know of a good firm.

4. You pay for the number of houses being delivered to in each suburb. Acreages are usually charged at a higher rate.

5. Best to get quotes and negotiate the price, which is often fluid.

You order various numbers of folded and unfolded flyers from the printer.

The printer will usually arrange for delivery of the folded flyers to the distributor or for the distributor to collect from the printer. In some cases you may need to do this.

Check arrangements with your printer and distributor. You will need to make similar arrangements with the printer for the unfolded flyers the PMM will need to distribute.

Producing a Flyer

An effective flyer is similar to a double paged advertisement.

It is not a good idea to leave one side blank when it is relatively inexpensive doing a second side. Not a good idea to let an opportunity go by.

You may like to do everything onsite or send all resources to the graphic artist at the printers for completion.

Production is similar to creating an advertisement but with more detail:

- Sketch layout outlines according to decided themes and branding

- Arrange photo placement. (Each photo need to be large enough to clearly see the required detail. Captions are not necessary, so the photo's message need to be very clear.)

- Write the text (e.g. Open Day text would need the details of the day including times, activities, displays, etc.)

- Select photos from your created file of photos for the year

- Arrange for the taking of any other photos you need

- Make final photo selections (Each photo tells a thousand words so be generous with these selections.)

- Discuss layout, texts and photos with the Parish Priest

- Include contact details for the parish, especially addresses, webaddress and phone number, at bottom of main page

- Proof all text

- Send sketches, pics and texts to printers for layout arranging (unless completed at the Parish Office or through a parishioner's generosity – then send digital file by email or CD)

- Proof drafts received back, usually by email from printers, with the Parish Priest or other key personnel. Send back to printers for updating.

- Read final draft and when all changes have been made sign-off for printing.

Reminder: Arrangements should have been made as to who will get the unfolded flyers to the CMM and the folded flyers to the letterbox distributors by the due dates.

Posters

> *Posters are usually large, colorful and effective forms of marketing.*

Creatively designed posters are eye-catching, attention-seeking advertisements.

Posters are best sized at double A3 i.e. A2

Strategically placed posters form an integral part of the CMP.

Effective Posters

Three effective posters, which do not rquire much preparation, are usually:

- Vision and Mission Statement

- Holy Week or Open Day (flyer)

- Information flyer (from the back of a previously produced flyer)

The Vision and Mission Statement should be displayed:

- throughout the parish and schools e.g. in the Parish and School Offices, in churches, etc.

Poster Display

The Holy Week / Open Day and Information flyers' Posters could be displayed at the front of each church, in the Parish Office, in the school's Front Office e.g. on notice boards or front doors, along with the Student Administration Office windows or student notice boards and at shopping centers.

All posters could be displayed at key events e.g. Open Day, Feast Day celebrations, Information Nights.

Posters are best laminated for effect and longevity.

The developmental production of these posters is the same as for the Flyers.

Brochures

Professionally produced brochures highlight specific aspects of the parish.

A good form of target marketing is through the use of brochures.

Key Brochures

The Parish Vision and Mission Statement should be presented in a brochure which is supported by posters.

Other key Brochures could include:

- Parish Staff and Specialist Support Staff – roles, general policies and offerings

- Sacramental Programs - details and personnel

- Social Justice, Welfare and Pastoral Care Programs and personnel

- Family support structures and programs

- Parish Pastoral Council - personnel including short biographies and role of Council

- Welcoming – general overview for new parishioners

- Deanery overview – supplied by deanery with each parish's input

Accessibility

The Brochures would need to be easily accessible. Some of the best forms of availability are:

- Inclusion in the Parish Information Kit

- Inclusion in the schools' prospectus

- In display / collection stands in the Parish's and Schools' Front Offices and at the front of each church

- From the key stakeholders e.g. Parish Priest / Priests / Pastoral Associates at interviews or visitations, Principals at enrolment interviews, School leaders at subject selection interviews, Parish and School Counselors

- At Open Days

- Information Nights

Other suggestions

- A good size is A4 folded into thirds along the long side.

- Branding is important, as is the layout.

- Be careful that the appearance isn't too busy i.e. cluttered.

- Wording should be succinct and informative.

- Once again brevity is important.

- Production is similar to a flyer but more detail is possible i.e. more text and more photos.

Signs and Sign Boards

Each church needs attractive, clearly visible signs stating the parish's name.

Along with other church details, as needed.

Church Signs

These need be displayed at key points around the parish's boundary.

The main entrance to the church should have the most significantly displayed sign.

If there is only one sign, it is probably best near the main entrance to the church. The church is for most people their main purpose for attendance in the parish.

Other directional signs could then direct people to other key facilities e.g. Parish Office, Presbytery, Parish Centre, Schools, Aged Care, Pre-School, etc.

The lettering should be relatively large and in keeping with the parish's branding style.

The church's name is sometimes accompanied by other permanent information on the same board e.g. worship times, motto, significant message or parish contact details.

If this is always the case at a particular parish, the parish must be careful not to detract from seeing the name clearly, when first looking at the sign.

Signs are primarily for locating the church or parish and need the parish name to stand out.

Marketing the parish on the same sign is of a secondary importance but still an important purpose.

Signboards

Signboards which allow for regular changing of content, and are placed in the most convenient locations for the target group to read, are good marketing forms for:

- Mass and other Sacramental and Worship times

- new and Regular Parishioners for upcoming events

- the Public for information about the parish and possibly at times about the school, particularly regarding enrolments.

Regular Updating of Signboards

These forms of information sharing require regular updating.

The sign can quickly become an eyesore and not looked at if information remains the same for periods longer than a week. This would also be the case if the sign rarely has anything written on it.

> Having the sign blank for a few days occasionally is a good change.
>
> Witty comments, or other pertinent quotes, also serve a purpose, at times.

A responsible staff member or parishioner should take charge for changing the board.

Usually a member of the parish leadership team is responsible for the content on display. This role could be delegated to another staff member.

Large Photographic Sign / Electronic Signboard

Both the large photographic sign and the electronic signboard have become popular.

These can be very successful, yet relatively high priced.

The content and layout are critical:

- colors and photos need to be appealing (remember branding)

- photos need to be eye-catching and pertinent to the theme/s

- key words and points are essential (sentences get lost)

- the challenge is to include all the key information and yet not allow for busyness but for BREVITY!

Professional Advice Sort

Due to the significant expense of this project, professional advice is critical.

Spend considerable time with the suppliers / manufacturers discussing every detail including:

- size
- cost
- use of this form of marketing
- what works
- what doesn't work
- possible layouts
- themes for your parish, etc.

Ask the suppliers for names of other parishes and schools you could speak with and approach these parishes and schools for further unbiased information.

Churches and Schools of the same denomination as yours are more likely to relate to your questions.

> Planning the layout, content, photos and aspects of branding to be used are similar to creating newspaper and magazine advertisements.

Promotional Items

Everyone loves a gift.
Promotional items are usually forms of gifts to new parishioners, their
children and guests to your parish.

Feel-Good Approach and Examples

Promotional items are a successful feel-good approach.

Children, particularly in elementary primary school, very much enjoy receiving these items.

The common successful forms are good quality and value:

- biros and pencils
- coffee cups
- drinking glasses
- rulers
- erasers
- fridge magnets
- calendar fridge magnets
- calculators
- stickers
- balloons.

However, the list of possibilities is quite considerable.

The cheaper forms are often placed in 'sample bags' for distribution along with the Parish Information Kit and inclusions to new parishioners during visits to their homes, at School Visitations and Parish and School Open Days.

The more expensive biros, calculators, cups and drinking glasses are often given to visiting dignitaries and guests. Some form of these often become part of the farewell gift to departing parishioners.

Suppliers

The cost and quality of these promotional items varies considerably.

Quotes should be obtained from a number of suppliers. It is a good practice to obtain quotes from reliable suppliers that other parishes, schools or the diocese uses.

> **Part of the quote will include the cost of graphics i.e. the set up costs for your logo and details which you want imprinted / etched on each item.**

The details you want inscribed on the items need to attract the reader to your church and include as many details as possible. Keeping these simple is best.

Often these are: logo, parish name, suburb, catch-phrase / motto, suburb, webaddress and telephone number. The minimum and often best practice is:

- parish name
- suburb
- webaddress
- phone number.

You can easily send all details via email.

Quantities are best ordered to last over 2-3 years.

The greater number ordered the better cost per unit ratio.

Items vary in cost but a varied selection ordered for over a year's supply will usually cost a few thousand dollars all up. Shop around.

Mid to Long Term Success

This marketing method also allows the church name to have a lasting place in the life of the child and family e.g.:

- fridge magnet on the fridge at home for the year

- biro and ruler being used at school or home

- mugs and glasses used at home or brought out on special occasions.

Parish Yearbook

Long-lasting, informative, interesting and a special record of the parish year.

Introduction

A number of parishes are now considering the benefits of a Parish Yearbook

(or a bi / tri annual production) or even a smaller yet enlarged commercially produced newsletter.

This is a special production which needs detailed planning.

The good length for a parish yearbook would be 20-40 pages necessary to gain a good overview of the year.

It should be a primary aim to include information and photos of as many parishioners as possible in the publication.

Graphic Artist

A good graphic artist will save on time, creativity and stress, considerably.

Engaging a graphic artist with experience in yearbooks is a great advantage.

This person will be paid in addition to the quotes from the printers, unless you use a printing firm with a graphic artist attached.

You may engage your normal printer's graphic artist also. This would often be better value for money.

This normal printing firm of yours would also have the added bonus of an electronic record and hence access to all your published photos and texts for the year/s.

Production Timeline

Production preparation of the Yearbook is often over most of the year.

Good planning would include realistic fixed due dates for content from:

- Parish Priest
- Priests
- Pastoral Associate
- Parish Manager
- School Principals
- Aged Care Director
- Preschool / Childcare Directors
- Group Leaders
- Chair of the Parish Pastoral Council
- Chair of the Finance Committee
- Other Committee Leaders, etc.

The staff needs to be aware of these dates.

A few follow-up reminders closer to their required due dates are essential.

Few people will be on time without follow-ups. Even then there will be some who still can't make it.

Allow some days in your planning for these sorts of people. Be willing to sit with them, collect ideas and produce a page for them.

Editor

The Yearbook Editor should best be someone other than the CMM, due to the time consuming nature of this production.

Interested and skilled parishioners working with the CMM could be a successful model. The CMM should usually take on a part time Editor / Publisher role here.

The Yearbook Editor will need very good organization skills, interpersonal skills, literary skills, have a creative flare and be prepared to work on a whole year project.

A well planned parish computer network would have the facility to store photos as soon as these are taken.

If this is the case, the Editor would explore photos when they are placed on the network by various members of the parish, evaluate the quality and position these would suit in the yearbook, and then store the photos in these particular folders on their computer.

Articles should be saved on the parish's network in designated folders as soon as these can possibly be written.

Leaving writing / collecting articles / photos etc to the last moment can cause time and production difficulties.
Recalling the full possible content of the event may also be lost due to the time since it occurred.

CMM and Editor

The requirements of this job are usually too big for the CMM. The CMM will need to oversee the production.

The CMM needs to be aware that getting in the way may backfire!

Be professional, plan early with the Yearbook Editor and lock in follow-up meetings throughout the year.

It is often good to meet at least at the beginning of each month to discuss updates and to evaluate the process.

A new Editor may need considerable assistance from the CMM and other staff.

Plan for Yearbook Editor:

- Be well prepared!!!

- View a number of other church's and schools' yearbooks for ideas

- Meet regularly with the CMM who acts as a sounding board and who is usually ultimately responsible for the production

- Keep in contact with the Parish Priest either directly or through the CMM

- Obtain quotes from a number of printers and graphic artists. Often best to use your own printing firm, if at all possible, as they usually have a good feel of your requirements, know how you work, have a number of photos and stories already, etc.

- Arrange with Graphic Artist to initially meet to discuss overall plan, timeline dates for him / her, etc. Discuss possible creative features of the production including overall theme / feel and specific page layouts e.g. class photo presentation style

- Plan regular meeting dates with the Graphic Artist throughout the year. Be aware not to overdo this though. Meeting each couple of months early on, and more often closer to publication date, is often sufficient, particularly if in contact through emails and telephone.

- Develop an overall plan in consultation with the CMM, page by page to cover all key aspects of the church / parish year book

- Decide which pages will be color. It is good to have at least 4 plus pages in color. The more you can afford the better.

- Have a clear, realistic timeline

- Disseminate the timeline to all people involved

- Discuss with key people what is required of them and when it is required by

- Select a unique front cover that says, "This is …. (Parish)." Less is best though. A busy front cover distracts.

- Have a separate folder in the Yearbook folder on your computer for each page of the Yearbook

- Add to these folders throughout the year when content and pics become available

- **Do not leave things to the last minute. Too much stress! Too much chance of failure!**

Give **reminders** nearer due dates!

- Branding needs inclusion throughout, *but not the same everywhere*, as this will overdo and become less interesting – work on variations, including waterwash, partial sections of logos and colors, similar but slightly different versions of the colors and symbols and at times no branding at all, just a plan page...

- Make arrangements to send groups of pages when all details have been collected to the Graphic Artist who then works creatively and sends back drafts for your consideration

- When pages are finalized send off to the printer for printing

- Remember that good printers will have numerous other jobs on the go when you require yours done.

> Therefore give the printing firm plenty of notice of your requirements and also send completed material to them when ready and when they would like it e.g. the Easter report and photos soon after these celebrations occur.

- Try not leaving key events out of the publication due to time constraints.

- Arrange with the printers and graphic artist to have these sent as soon as possible after the agreed event/s have occurred if these are close to publication date.

Church Marketing and the Traditional Media+ Instructions

Church Marketing and the Traditional Media + Instructions

Do not fear the media but be prepared!

All you are ever likely to need to know about dealing successfully with the media.

This Chapter will help you deal with the journalists, photojournalists and media outlets to gain the best results for your church / parish.

You are in charge but need to appreciate the role these people play in marketing your church / parish.

The big challenges of writing media releases and editorials (stories) are clearly explained here. There is a sample to view!

Headings

- Media
- Media Releases
- Writing a Media Release (+ Sample)
- Media Interview
- Journalists Visit Parish
- Photojournalists at Parish
- Editorial from the Parish (+ Sample)
- The Difficult Media Situation
- Staged' events

Traditional Media

The traditional media - newspapers, magazines, radio, television - still has a powerful influence on people's perceptions of churches and parishes.

Effectively using the media is of considerable advantage.
(It is also of benefit to the media.)

Do not be afraid of the media! Be respectful!

A common misconception is that the media will contact the church / parish on a regular basis for stories. Most often this is not the case.

When a good relationship is developed between the church / parish and the various media outlets, a balance and appreciation of each other's needs will be reached.

Positive Relations

Parishes need to develop positive relations with the media. Having the media work for you is a real advantage.

Also, having the media not work against you is another advantage.

Most media outlets want to work with churches to portray positive stories to their readers. These are the feel-good stories, which sell newspapers, television and radio time.

This builds the media's advertising base, hence profits.

They are also seen as good community advocates.

This positive relationship doesn't just happen.

The Church Marketing Manager, in particular, needs to develop this relationship in a number of ways.

These include contact with journalists, good media releases, advertising with them and the availability of the PMM to the media outlet.

Church Contact Person

- **The CMM should be the known contact person for the media.**

To avoid confusion the media should be channeled through the CMM even though the issues may concern another staff member or parishioner. Parish Office personnel and other staff need to be aware of this.

The media would usually prefer to contact one person for ease.

- **Confusion may lead to unforeseen results.**

Confusion may exist when this doesn't occur. Sometimes the media get annoyed with perceived buck-passing.

Sometimes the parish may get 'tricked', or not be fully aware of the line of enquiry, by a section of the media following up on a less than positive perceived or real story. This may occur when the media engages someone from the parish who does not know how to deal with them or what should be released by the parish on a particular issue.

The only exception should be a request to speak with the Parish Priest / Pastor, as long as they are content with this procedure. Often the Parish Priest will seek the CMM's advice or that of the Diocesan Communications and Marketing Manager before completing the media's request.

> The Parish Priest needs to make his role in certain media requests clear to the CMM to avoid any confusion.

Media Release

The CMM needs to provide stories to the media which they would want to run. This initially is given in the form of a media release. Follow-up telephone calls often assist the process.

The CMM should cultivate particular contacts within each media organization to follow up the media releases. (See 'Writing the Media Release')

Direct Contact with Media Outlets and Journalists

There are also certain types of stories for particular outlets. A sample of this would be the feature pages within a newspaper. These features often cover community activities in general and cover a wide variety of themes e.g. sport, the arts, literature reviews, community service activities and articles of interest to their readers.

These types of stories need a specific contact with that features subeditor, or journalist, and not a media release. A phone call from the CMM initially ascertains if there is particular interest in a suggestion. This is followed by further calls, emails, possible interviews and photo sessions, as needed, as the project develops.

> Having journalists who you can bounce ideas off to decide what is of interest will invariably save time and gain a wider media acceptance of your ideas and the stories presented.

This further enhances your reputation with these journalists and the success rate for having stories covered.

Balanced Relationship is Needed

A balance is needed in appreciating how much contact you should make via media releases and direct contact to journalists.

A problem develops when your media releases or phone calls become intrusive and overbearing. No-one wants to be harassed and journalists may feel this way if a balance on the amount of contact isn't reached.

> Sometimes it is a good idea to place yourself in their shoes.

How much contact for gaining stories would you like? Remember that you are not the only one with stories. Also, the subeditor has other expectations of the journalist and his / her need to meet these.

CMM's Availability

> The CMM should always give a response to a particular request immediately.

However, you do not need to give the answers to their questions immediately.

Your response may be that you will get back to them shortly with their request. Make sure this happens within a reasonable time limit, say 30 minutes.

Often you will need to arrange for one of the priests, chair of the parish pastoral council or parishioners to be available for an interview and photo session. Or it may be for these people, or a specific staff member, to answer a few questions in an interview either face to face or over the telephone.

Most stories the media wishes to cover can be arranged within a day or two. Sometimes this will need to be arranged in a couple of hours.

Be Careful – Do Not Seem Uninterested

If the media outlet feels as though you are not available or lack interest, they will go to another parish or source for their request.

Each media outlet will have a short list of parishes they will contact if they need a church's input or photo for a story. This list will change depending on the support given by those parishes to the media's requests.

The Media Release

The media release is your way of informing the media of something special.

When Used

Mostly it is used to try to get coverage for a particular event or success about to occur, occurring, or recently occurred, within the church.

Sometimes it is used to advise the media of information necessary to allay any negative stories.

No Guarantees

There is no guarantee that the media will be interested in covering your story.

It is not easy getting the media to run your stories. There is much news out there and there are many parishes and church schools vying for media space.

This may appear harsh, however if it was a 'big news' day your story may have been small in comparison. You may try again when a similar story occurs.

Experience will help you evaluate those stories which have more chance of successfully being picked up by various media outlets.

DO NOT GIVE UP!

Better Chances of Coverage

At least there will be times when there is that quiet news day when the media is looking for something within reason!

Keep your relationship with the media growing so that you will be considered, especially for these types of days.

The Christmas and summer holidays are a good time to get coverage. This is usually a quiet news time.

There will be times when you have a good success rate and other times when it seems that no matter what you offer no outlet is interested.

Long Dry Periods - Response

If the dry period is too long you will need to develop other forms of media communication or expand on already used ones.

An example of this would be to write your own newsletter, and professionally produce this newsletter / booklet. A good size is A4 of about 12 to 16 pages in length. (See more details on this form of 'do-it-yourself' publication in 'Commercially Produced Newsletter' section).

Another option would be for you to enhance your weekly e/i-newsletter or newsletter and / or increase its distribution list.

Don't forget the e/i-type of publication where you email out or have the publication placed on your webpage! (See e/i-Newsletter / Newsletter section in Resources portfolio.)

Advertising usually gains certain amounts of editorial space for certain sized adverts in various features in newspapers.

The feature sections are often pullout sections. Feature sections which often assist parishes could be: Lifestyle, Community Service or Education.

The space allowed for editorial is usually in a 50/50 ratio if you use a certain sized larger advertisement. These advertisements are measured in column centimetres: so many columns wide by so many centimeters deep. Check with your outlets. (See 'Editorial from the Parish' section.)

'The Event' - Two Media Releases

Two media releases are often found to be the best approach for each event that is about to occur and which you would like to have covered.

The first is sent a day or two before for a normal event. However, you may need to send it a week before for a major big story event e.g. 50th anniversary of the parish or new facility opening.

> **The first media release gives details necessary to gain interest.**

This hopefully gains a telephone request from the media for more details or for an interview and / or photo request.

The second media release should be sent very early on the day of the event - best before 8am.

This gives more detail and acts as an enticement.

> **The second media release also repeats in a different way the main points from the first media release and adds necessary new information.**

The second media release needs to emphasise the logistics of when, where and who is involved.

You may also need to follow-up the 'big event' media release with a call to your contacts in the various outlets or to the outlets in general requesting to speak with a journalist re a recently sent media release regarding a major event.

Writing the Media Release + Sample

Media Release Writing Skills

Develop effective Media Release writing skills so as to gain media coverage.

This is often your best means of gaining this somewhat difficult exposure.

The media release should ideally be kept to one page to be effective. (See Sample at end of this chapter.)

One of the major difficulties found when beginning to write media releases is keeping the length relatively short.

There is often a desire to give all the detail because you believe it enhances your case.

Sometimes a little more detail is needed, but not to the detriment of the success of the media release.

You may also attach supporting documentation. Supporting documentation is usually better than an extended release. It breaks up a long media release.

A media release is often read if the heading and introduction is captivating.

Long releases can be considered boring and hence not read.

Remember that the media outlets are receiving an enormous number of releases daily.
The best media releases and best stories usually gain the best attention.

Sending a Media Release

- The media release is printed onto the church's letterhead paper before transmission.

- The media release is next faxed or emailed to the chosen media outlets.

- In most cases this is to a list of media outlets which should have been stored prior in the memory of the fax machine's / email group list.

- Emailing is currently gaining more of a general acceptance from the media for media releases. You need to know each outlet's expectations.

- If they are not email interested, you may still be able to arrange emails with specific contacts for certain focused stories e.g. community service feature pages within the local newspaper.

- Follow-up phone calls may need to be made if there is no response or if you just want to keep building on your relationship. Remember not to overdo this though.

Response of Media to an Event

- Media representatives will usually contact you if there is an interest.

- The media may not always respond to your media release but may just turn up a few minutes before the event ready to do the coverage.

- Have someone prepared to meet them in the Parish Office if you know they will be there or have some other contingency plans just in case they arrive without you knowing.

- Be courteous and welcoming, have them sign in and then taken to the venue. They should then be introduced to the CMM who then helps them out.

Suggested Media Release Outline Plan:

- On parish letterhead stationery

- Banner stating: <u>MEDIA RELEASE</u> (in very large, bold letters e.g. 72 point size)

- Date below stating: <u>For immediate release: List Date</u> (in large letters e.g. 22 point size).

  (You always have the right to place an embargo on the release to a later specified date. However, from a parish's point of view, this would hardly, if ever, occur. If an embargo is placed on the release date of the story write this embargoed date:

  <u>Embargoed release: List Date</u>)

- Heading in large, bold letters (about 22 point size). Keep it as brief as possible. The heading should immediately capture the reader's attention, such that they wish to read on.

- Bulk of release: Needs to be in order of priority of points. Main points at the beginning and lesser points at end, in normal 12 point font size.

- The lead paragraph is critical to gaining attention. It should be your main point.

- **The reader at the media outlet will only read what they find interesting. If you leave important points to the end of the media release these might not get read because the reader may have stopped reading and already disposed of your media release.**

- The release should be written in succinct short paragraphs, often in single sentences for effect.

- Quotes from key people should most often be included. These would usually come from the Parish Priest and other key people noted in the release. Best to have no more than two people quoted, but preferably only one. This saves on confusion and the release becoming too wordy.

- End with: .../end

- If the request is for the media's presence at an event, etc, repeat or highlight at the end of the media release in a separate succinct sentence in bold type the key details which tell the journalist where and when they need to be at a particular venue.

- Below this add the details of who authorized the media release and contact details including mobile / cell number and email address. Without this the release has no real authority and no-one to contact. Remember, you are hoping for a visit on the day of the event or contact for success.

Sample follows next page...

(NB - On Church Letterhead Document)

Media Release

For immediate release: 3 April, 2011

Major Easter Re-enactment for Church and School Tomorrow at 10am

Easter celebrations begin at [Parish Name, Suburb] tomorrow with the dramatic annual Easter Celebration for our school children. The re-enactment depicts significant moments in the last days of the life of Jesus.

Both the church and school grounds will be used. Palm Sunday begins in the Middle School Area, the Last Supper, Trial and 39 Lashes in the School Assembly Area, the Crucifixion at the Drama Centre and the Resurrection in [Church name] Church.

Over 60 students are directly involved as actors, dancers, musicians and singers. The remainder of the College jeers during the trial and places colorful flowers on the cross at the resurrection. A spectacular freeze of Jesus in the arms of Mary at the foot of the cross under red lights occurs in the Drama Centre after the crucifixion.

"This spectacular liturgy is a wonderful way for the [School name] community to begin their Easter celebrations. The students' involvement is something special to see," said [Name], Parish Priest.

The liturgy begins in the College Assembly Area at 10am and concludes in the [Name] Church around 11:30am

Many unique photo opportunities exist.

Authorized by: [Name], Church Marketing Manager

[Telephone and email contact detail]

The Media Interview

Be well prepared!

> The media interview is a very important means of getting your message across to an outside media outlet.
>
> Again - Be well prepared!

The interview is usually conducted by a journalist at the church or parish centre / office.

Sometimes over-the-phone interviews occur.

Who is interviewed?

The Parish Priest is mostly interviewed. Sometimes other priests, pastoral associate or the parish pastoral council chair may be interviewed. Sometimes the CMM is the delegated person.

Each church needs to clarify who will be interviewed under various circumstances to avoid misunderstandings or confusion within the church and outside with the media outlet.

The CMM may be interviewed for clarification of facts being needed by the journalist for a particular story or upcoming interview. The CMM may be asked to give quick quotes for the completion of a story or for an addition to a news story requiring a parish's input.

The CMM may need to seek the Parish Priest's input for these types of quotes.

The CMM may need to obtain a quote from the Parish Priest.

Preparation for the interview

Parish representatives need to be well prepared for any interview.

> **If possible, practice interviews should be conducted before the journalist arrives.**
>
> **The CMM should pre-empt possible questions for those being interviewed.**

Even if the interviewee is the only person who knows the detail being sort, the CMM's preparedness is required.

Go over with the interviewee what the procedure will be and possible questions.

The CMM needs to build confidence in the person about to be interviewed.

This is best done through thorough preparation. People feel more confident when questioned on areas for which they are prepared.

> **Concentrating on the key 3-4 points you want to get across is often the best and easiest way of approaching the preparation and interview.**

> However, it is also necessary to try and pre-empt possible 'curly' questions and develop possible responses.

Prior to the journalist arriving, the CMM should make firm plans with those to be interviewed to meet at a designated time and at a designated place. This allows the CMM to ascertain whether everyone is present and if any last minute change of arrangements is required.

Sometimes the journalist is late.

This is unfortunate; however it is best to make plans to suit the journalists for as soon as they are able to arrive. This sometimes causes great inconvenience to the parish, interviewees and CMM.

Sometimes either the journalist or photojournalist arrives at different times. This isn't usually a problem as it is possible to start with just one present.

Conducting the Interview:

- The CMM would meet the journalist and often a photojournalist at the parish office. Welcome them appropriately and have them sign in. They may need to wear parish endorsed name tags while in the parish grounds.

- Offer them a non-alcoholic drink.

- Have a predetermined venue on offer, whether indoors or outdoors depending on the nature of the story and weather conditions at that moment. Offer this suggestion to the journalist who will usually accept.

- Have a chat about where you are about to go, the interviewees involved and any restrictions e.g. time restrictions that may be apparent.

- The CMM then takes the journalists and interviewees to the selected venue/s.

- If some photos are being taken at the same time as some interviews, the CMM will need to arrange for another well informed staff member to assist the photojournalist.

- The CMM, or any designated staff member, should usually remain with the journalists until they leave the parish grounds.

CMM at Interview

- The CMM must maintain control over the interview situation but in a quiet, non-threatening way.

- The CMM, or a well informed staff member designate, needs to be present at all interviews with young people. The main reason is as a duty of care. It is beneficial to be present at staff interviews also.

- The CMM's presence helps the young person or staff member be more at ease through having a supportive staff member at the interview.

- The CMM may also be called upon by either party for assistance or clarification.

- The interviewee needs to appreciate that the interview is to be conducted for a positive outcome.

  - Only positive points should be discussed.

Negative Questions – A Response Method

Anticipate the sort of negative questions which might arise and prepare good responses.

Have your key 3 positive points you would like to make.

Key techniques during the interview are:

1. Acknowledge the weakness (apologize if needed)

2. Agree that plans are afoot to improve the situation

3. Continually revert back to the 3 key positive points you want to make

---

It may also be necessary to make arrangements with the interviewee prior to the interview, and before the journalist arrives, that the CMM would interject respectfully if the interviewee was getting particularly stressed or confused during the interview.

An example could be that if the interviewer says that it must get frustrating having very few parishioners attending liturgies, then it may be necessary to remind the interviewee that it could appear so but that the benefits of all this hard work in creating better liturgies will assist with the growth in the numbers of participants. Better liturgies will attract more parishioners.

It is often best to do this in a light-hearted manner and preferably in a fun way.

Journalists Visiting the Parish

As a general rule, the CMM or designate should always be with the journalists while they are in the parish grounds.

Meeting Time

The CMM needs to be accurate with the time given for the journalists to be present e.g. advise that the function starts at 6pm, the guest speaker will speak at 6:10pm and the speaker will be available for interview at 7pm.

Journalists' schedules are often tight, which means they have a specific time to leave for their next appointment.

The interview time arranged needs to be met.

They should be welcomed, signed-in if necessary and offered a non-alcoholic drink. They will often not accept these unless they are early or the event / interview are late and they have some leeway time.

Coverage of an Event and CMM's Role

Until a good rapport with various journalists is developed, it is best for the CMM or designate to be with them while they are in the church's grounds covering specific events.

The CMM or designate should always be present with the journalist or photojournalist at interviews and photo taking.

The designate would need a thorough briefing beforehand on their role, what they should do and possibly some of the things that they should say.

It is suggested that you do not take anything for granted in assuming this designated person knows what to do.
You need to fully inform him / her.

Once a rapport is developed over time, the journalists are most likely capable of being trusted to move around appropriately to listen, video or take pictures of these events e.g. various liturgies or functions, etc.

If an interview or a posed photo is required after the event, the CMM or designate needs to be present.

This allows him / her to maintain control, help with setting up for photos or interviews and assist those about to be interviewed.

The CMM is also a supportive presence and someone who can usually allay the nerves of those involved.

**The CMM should not let the journalists do anything s/he is not happy about.
You have a right to step in if necessary.**

You may be responsible for the young people or students in your care and hence those being interviewed or photographed may need your assistance.

Be reasonable though, remembering that the journalists are doing their job and in most cases are on your side.

Know your legal and ethical responsibilities.

Seek these from qualified legal practitioners and ethicists.

Photojournalists

Overview

Photojournalists are responsible for getting the best photos they can for their particular media outlets.

Photojournalists will most likely have good ideas to best represent the image you want covered.

The CMM, or selected well informed staff member, need to attend all photo sessions.

Photo sessions are usually enjoyable times for all involved. It is not often that people appear in the media. The CMM should treat it as an enjoyable time and it most likely will end up being so.

The photojournalist usually works with the journalist who is covering the story. Yet it is often the photojournalist who decides which photos will be used.

There will be times when the media outlet only wants a photo and just sends a photojournalist.

At other times you will need to arrange for interviews and photos at the same or similar times.

However, at other times, the interview may happen over the telephone and the photo taken at a separate time.

Even though most stories require a photo, sometimes it is not required.

Own Parish Photos

There may also be times when the media outlet is quite happy for you to send your own photos by email instead of having the photojournalist come out.

> This usually happens after the outlet appreciates the quality and content of your parish's photos and the professionalism of your photographers.

This is more common with the smaller publications, or for photos accompanying editorial in special features and for advertising.

Rest assured that the outlets will invariably send out a photographer if you feel you need one.

CMM and the Photojournalist

You are free to offer suggestions, though the final decision does rest with the photojournalist.

Their employer is their media outlet (and not your parish) and hence the photo taken is what they want.

However, in most cases the photojournalist is working with you and for the parish to be seen in the best light.

It is in their best interests to work with you for many reasons, including the media outlet's need for a good standing in the religious and wider community. They will also possibly want photos, reactions or stories from your parish down the track.

However, if you are being unfairly obstructive, then follow-up photos for other stories at other times may be few and far between.

Stopping Inappropriate Photos and Follow-Up

> **You must make sure that the photos taken are appropriate for parishioners of all ages, particularly for young people.**
>
> **Do not allow for anything raunchy or what might appear inappropriate.**

It is strongly suggested that parishioners in the photo shouldn't:

- hold any inappropriate prop e.g. cigarette
- appear before an inappropriate backdrop e.g. toilet or certain signage
- wear inappropriate clothing e.g. skimpy tops or skirts
- be positioned in any inappropriate manner e.g. sitting inappropriately.

> **If you are not happy with the photojournalist's suggestions, then stop the photo shoot, negotiate a better outcome, or cancel it.**
>
> **You are responsible for trying to get the best most appropriate photo.**

You have every right to do this; in fact you may have a responsibility to do this.

Advise your Parish Priest of this situation and outcome.

> **Know your legal and ethical responsibilities.**
>
> **Seek these from qualified legal practitioners and ethicists.**

If the photo session was cancelled, you or your Parish Priest would seriously consider contacting the media outlet's editor and advising of the inappropriateness of the photojournalist's expectations / demands. This should sort the problem out.

Further courses of action, if no success in the first instance was gained from the editor, would often be to contact your diocesan's Communication and Marketing Manager for guidance and support. Either your Parish Priest or the Communication and Marketing Manager would probably take the matter further e.g. journalists' association, members of parliament, etc and even to police / court if there was any abuse. This would be a very rare indeed.

Editorial from the Parish + Sample

When Needed

Throughout the year you will be required to write editorial for various media outlets.

This is more than likely the result of the provision of free editorial with certain sized advertisements in special newspaper or magazine features.

Due to the number of parishes, schools and other community organisations trying to gain media attention, for most parishes free editorial accompanying paid feature advertisements would be the only way of having editorial published.

Rarely, it may be the result of an invitation from the media outlet e.g. 50th anniversary of the parish or for Holy Week. Usually these events would be covered by media releases or as a part of a paid advertising package.

What is editorial?

Editorial is the 'story' component in the media outlet's production.

At times you may be asked to provide editorial i.e. a story to usually accompany an advertisement of a certain size, along with photo/s. (See Sample Below.)

The editorial is similar to a media release on the selected theme/s but with more of an advertising component. The media outlets normally allow for these to be virtually advertorials i.e. an advertising editorial. You would be promoting your parish.

It is written in the same format as a media release (see 'Writing a Media Release').

It is often longer than a media release, therefore has more content and detail.

The space available will often match the space the advertisement takes.

You will also need to allow for a photo. Editorial is boring without a photo.

Remember that a photo 'tells thousands of words'.

The photo is normally selected from one or more that you send to the outlet.

Most outlets will send a photographer or photojournalist if you would rather this.

Advertisements Without Editorial

Placing advertisements outside special feature sections of publications i.e. in the body of the paper, or below the required size for gaining editorials as part of a feature's section, will generally not have the option of including editorials.

Way to Gain Editorial?

If you are a good advertising client or the paper needs to fill space, you may gain the occasional free editorial. This is very rare though.

Steps for Creating Editorial:

- The media outlet would contact you once you have confirmed the booking of an appropriate sized advertisement as part of a feature section.

- The contacting journalist will be either from the media outlet or from a journalist consultancy company. The outside consultants do the work of a normal journalist and then send the finished product to that outlet.

- You will be usually asked to provide details for them to create a story for you. You will also be asked for a time for them to send a photographer / photojournalist to the parish. They are prepared to do as much as possible for you.

- The details you send are best sent in the format of a media release. This allows the journalist to see your priorities and the emphasis you would like to make. When you gain experience in media release writing for editorial, you will often find that the journalist will select much of your release verbatim. This is a real credit to you and an advantage to the parish because the message you wanted published for the community has been achieved.

- The number of words required varies and you will normally be advised of this. If not, you should ask for the number. You need to keep fairly close to this word count.

- However, if you go beyond the requested number of words and your content is very good, and space is available, you may gain a longer published story. Best not count on this as it is the exception and not the rule.

Photos

With experience you will know the types of photos that best suit certain stories and which would be acceptable to the outlet.

If there is a photo you really want published, and it is of the quality required of the media outlet, then just send it. They will advise if it doesn't suit and discuss other options with you.

If unsure, it is best to send a small selection, say 3-4 photos, which you would be happy to have published, and allow the journalist to decide.

Offer captions to explain each photo. (See sample below.)

(On Parish stationery - Fictional sample)

New DVD Shows the Uniqueness of the Southport Parish

Staff and students of Aquinas College produced a new parish DVD which gives a dynamic and honest view of the uniqueness of the Southport Parish.

Fr Peter Dillon, Parish Priest, began the DVD emphasizing the welcoming and respectful nature of the Parish and what it offers people within its personnel's care.

"The Southport Parish is dynamic, offering something unique for everyone from birth to death. From birth blessings and family prayer in the hospital ward to prep, primary and secondary education, adult and family groups, welfare and pastoral care programs, to the elderly and aged care homes and facilities, all on the one precinct, are quite unique," said Fr Peter Dillon, Parish Priest.

Mrs. Maryanne Finder, Principal of the secondary Aquinas College, followed briefly highlighting her school.

"Aquinas College offers a quality, Catholic education for all our students. As stated in our Vision and Mission statement, we value a welcoming community where students are safe, happy, can learn and are treated with respect," said Mrs. Finder, Principal.

Video images of the Parish are used throughout the DVD to show many outstanding aspects of daily and sacramental life.

High Christian values are emphasized by Fr Peter as the cornerstone of this very successful parish.

"Our relationships are built on integrity and compassion, justice and mercy, forgiveness and love."

The new DVD is part of the 'Welcome to Southport Parish' and the 'Southport Parish is for You' kits. It is also part of the enrolment packages at both schools and may be obtained by ringing the College on [number] and Guardian Angels School on [number] or emailing the Parish Secretary at: [email address of parish]

Pic 083: Fr Peter Dillon supervising the final editing of the DVD in the Film and Television studio at Aquinas College

Pics 022 and 026: College Captains [Names] during videoing of the new Aquinas College DVD. (Preference is for one of these two.)

Pic 027: Year 8 student [Student name] during videoing of the new Aquinas College DVD

Authorized by: Name, Role, Southport Parish phone / fax / mobile or cell, email address.

The Difficult Media Situation

Sometimes the media request an interview with no forewarning.
This usually happens when a story is considered 'big' and difficult.

Overview

This may be when something controversial or of a significant status has occurred and the media wants to run with that story on that day or the next.

Examples of these would include:

- a disaster where the church or parish centre has had major damage, such as from a major storm or fire
- a staff member or school employee has been allegedly involved with something illegal
- a former staff member or school student has done something highly successful, controversial or allegedly illegal
- the government or local council have or will make a decision that impacts significantly on the church, parish, school, etc.

Parish Response

In this case initially you need to advise the media that the parish representative, through the parish priest, yourself or someone else, will speak with them shortly.

You have every right to consider your options before speaking.

It is often best to contact the diocesan Communications and Marketing Manager, if such a role exists. This manager is usually familiar with best practice for such events. The manager will either become directly involved and speak on behalf of the parish or offer suggestions on the best approach. The manager may also contact others within or outside the diocese who may be able to offer advice e.g. lawyers, building or insurance advisors / consultants, counsellors, etc.

Offering a "No comment" is often fraught with potential misinterpretation or even worse. The outlet could, in this situation, just take the story according to the information they have, which may not be the truth or whole truth.

Comment truthfully.
You do not need to give all the details but offer what is needed for the media enquiry allowing for privacy and ethical considerations.

This may be just a simple, "Thank you for the enquiry. We will get back to you shortly."

If the parish decides to act on the request itself there are a number of approaches which should benefit the parish:

- Be available for an interview in person or over the phone.

- Be positive and in control during the interview

- Appearance is important e.g. appropriate demeanour, dress, stance

- Control the backdrop for television or newspaper photo to get the positive visual message out that you want

- Answer all questions, but turn the answer to what you want to emphasize

- Having 3 key points to direct to the media is a good approach

- State the obvious, such as:

    * no one was hurt / unfortunately some people were injured
    * damage to the property was significant / minimal
    * the most important thing is that no-one was hurt, only property damage occurred and that this will be repaired as soon as possible or
    * unfortunately some people were hurt and the parish is currently doing everything possible for those people e.g. ambulance was called immediately, there will be ongoing medical assistance, a counsellor involved for those directly affected, other counselors are coming from sister parishes, etc.
    * the parish priest is sorry that this unfortunate event occurred, all procedures have been followed and that everything possible will be done to ensure that this won't happen again. If updating procedures is necessary then this will be done immediately.

Criminal Matters

For potential criminal matters refer the media to a specific contact at the diocesan level (who you have forewarned and briefed in detail) who would be best placed to deal with that situation.

Follow-up

Be available to keep the media updated as the situation changes or developments are made.

Keep well advised, especially from the diocesan level.

For criminal matters follow the diocesan advice throughout the whole process.

Staff Preparation for Interviews

- Personnel who will appear on television, radio or within print should practise the skills needed to be successful. It can be quite daunting when someone with a camera or microphone requests you to speak.

- You need to appear to be coherent, informed and in control. It is even more confronting when there are a number of cameras, microphones and people standing before you, particularly if it is due to a serious nature.

- **Practise, practise, practise your interview techniques.**

Use video cameras and audio recording devices to record your responses and then learn from your experiences.

Have selected staff members act as journalists and have them interview you.

Allow for the difficult questions because this is part of the process.

Remember, to keep coming back to your 3 key positive points. Be as positive as possible.

'Staged' Events

A number of events may be 'staged' for optimum media / marketing coverage throughout the year.

Defined

These events would most often be special / different / controversial / outstanding parish events which would be heavily marketed, with a primary marketing aim of gaining some media coverage.

The secondary aim is usually something special for the parish.

The desired media involvement would be free coverage gained as a result of media releases and / or phone calls to key media people.

Main Events

The main events for most parishes are:

- special celebrations done very well or differently e.g. Holy Week, Christmas and Parish Feast Day
- 'Parish Open Days'
- major social / social justice / prayerful occasions
- arrival of a new PP
- special donations / community involvement

Try something very different e.g. Phone-a-thon or a unique Liturgy. Two examples I have done follow:

1. The Phone-a-thon was set up with the local television station and went live to air during and after the local news and weather segments. The purpose was to track down past students from the College for an upcoming major school anniversary. The setting was a small room with a number of key people, including the Principal, a past Principal, staff member, student and School Marketing Manager - all with

telephones. The SMM asked people to ring in details and also had a little 'chat' about the event with the host. The whole promotion went very well and was free of charge. It promoted the school and parish well and received considerable response from the public.

2. The College Easter Liturgy is still covered yearly by the local television station and major newspaper. Its significance is its size, number of students in costume or otherwise involved, scenes and props used throughout the school campus and local church, and vision of whole school being involved with each new station of the cross. The Principal, students or SMM, are interviewed by various media outlets each year.

Something Different

You might like to try:

- Being brave and prepared to hear from the general public suggestions to improve church / parish life and liturgical involvement and being open to receiving all sorts of positive but also confronting 'suggestions'

- taking a social justice stance on a key issue and going to the public for support - encouraging attendance at information sessions given by special guests / personalities, letter writing, protests, prayer vigils, etc.

- tracking down past parishioners for a 50th / 75th / 100th anniversary, etc.

Other Possible Events

- Parish Recognition Night (awards for special endeavors throughout the year...)
- Bishop's visit, linked to something unique within the parish / community
- Parish Musical, especially if a character is someone of note or unique
- Parish Feast Day
- School Graduation day
- Parish Dinner and special after dinner speaker
- Parish sports grand final game

> The event, or aspects / moments within it, should be as unique as possible to gain media attention. The staged event then becomes the focus of a marketing campaign.

Church Marketing Advertising in the Traditional Media

Church Marketing Advertising in the Traditional Media

Advertising in the media is an area many churches need to seriously consider. When done properly it is a very effective form of advertising.

This chapter will introduce you to these various forms of advertising and most importantly in simple to read points show how to go about creating advertisements for each form.

Being well prepared with background material and prepared to oversee the production and / or final advertisement presentation is necessary for success. This chapter will explain how to do all this in simple easy to read ways.

Headings

Advertising in the Media
Newspaper and Magazine Advertising
Creating a Newspaper or Magazine Advertisement
Radio Advertising
Creating a Radio Advertisement (+ Sample)
Television Advertising
Creating a Television Advertisement

Advertising in the Traditional Media

> This form of advertising is for a broad reach within society.
>
> It goes well beyond the parish community.

Common forms include: newspaper, radio, television and magazines.

Purpose and Overview

This form of advertising is mainly used to:

- Reach a broad audience beyond the parish community
- Build a reputation within the broader community
- Have the reputation created support those within the parish community
- Advise the broader community of the advantages of your church community
- Encourage others within the broader community to consider visiting and engaging more permanently within the parish community.

Success rates will vary depending on each individual publication and geographical location.

Advertising costs will also vary according to each individual publication and location.

Thorough cost analysis needs to be done by the CMM prior to developing a Church Marketing Plan (CMP).

Often the smaller more localized publications are the best value as they often cost less and usually reach the targeted audience more effectively. However, you need to be satisfied about:

- outlet's philosophy
- usual content
- style of presentation
- advertisement placement positions
- distribution method.

Advertisement Creation Options

- **Two options are usually available:**

  - The Church creates and produces its own advertisement or
  - The media outlet creates it for you

Each media outlet would normally create the advertisement for you, if you so wish. You should provide as much information and as many resources as possible, particularly the branding style needed (see 'Branding').

Don't expect this method to be thoroughly to your liking though. You may need to go back and forth with the outlet until satisfied.

- **Background preparation**

> **A database of resources is best to be created prior to the CMP's advertising campaign each year.**

This database would include, where possible:

- Themes
- Layout designs
- Photographs
- Advert wordings
- Parish contact details

Uniformity, according to the decided branding style, is essential for each advertisement.

For a new CMM in the early stages it might take some time to develop the database as you discover what works successfully.

- **Be prepared**

It is best not to leave it to the last minute to decide on photographs, etc. This would often result in a rushed and unsuccessful decision.

A 'hit and miss' style of advert designs is to be avoided!

Flexibility is also needed to allow for any changing circumstances.

- **Check Proofs**

You will need to thoroughly check and change anything which is not suitable in the proof / draft version. You are the client and have every right to make necessary changes. You will be respected for this accuracy. It also adds to the parish's reputation.

- **Sign-off on Advertisements**

  - Each advertisement you agree on will usually require two sign-offs:

    * When the advertisement booking is made
    * Agreeing to the final draft of the advertisement.

  - The sign-off is done by the person in authority at in your parish. The CMM would normally be this person who is appointed by the Parish Priest / Pastor.

  - These are contractual documents. Be completely happy with the details before signing-off.

  - Signing-off may be done by email e.g. the radio station sends the final recordings for your approval and you reply by email giving permission for the radio adverts to be run, according to the recordings sent.

Specific Examples Follow...

Newspaper and Magazine Advertising

Newspaper Advertising

Often this is the most popular form of paid advertising used by churches.

It is a relatively easy form of advertising for the CMM once the background preparation is done.

Planning

As part of the CMP, it is a good method to have the themes for each advertisement's placement throughout the year decided at the beginning of the year. This will allow for appropriate photos to be taken and copy (text to be used) considered well in advance.

Each time an advert is published, ask the outlet to email you the final copy for signing-off and for your records. This also assists with future advertising requirements and ideas.

Effectiveness

The effectiveness of this form of advertising is debatable.

Using the smaller forms of newspapers will often get the greatest result of readers per dollar spent.

The free 'throw over the fence' or 'letterbox' local paper meets this criterion the best. Because every household normally receives one, there is a good chance that a good readership size results. However, at what depth? Is it just skimmed? As it is free with no financial contribution from the reader, is the reader less inclined to spend quality time reading?

The larger city, state and national newspaper publications are much more expensive and usually have a smaller readership of your targeted audience. Yet the readership has decided to purchase the paper and hence is highly likely to read it.

Carefully selected newspaper advertising could be quite cost effective for a number of advertisements over the year, particularly considering the limited number most churches would do.

It is best to also do your own research on the readership and styles of your targeted readers.

Prestige

The other aspect worth considering is that of prestige.

Some churches would see the prestige value more important than the actual number of readers. If a church is looking for a more middle class demographic then it would more than likely want to be seen in a more prestigious publication i.e. a paper where there is a higher cost associated and a higher educated readership.

Solid Advertising Account Advantage

Having a solid advertising account will at times be to your advantage. Financially you will gain a decent discount.

Initially, an obvious point is that the more you advertise the greater number of people will read your advertisement and therefore more people will be informed about your parish.

It will also impose significantly on your Church Marketing Budget (CMB).

Positively though, you will more than likely gain in editorial / story space.

> **As in any business, the proprietors will assist their best clients.**
>
> **If your church is in this category, you would hope for more stories from your church being published.**

> You would also like to think that your church would be approached for a church's perspective on other particular stories.
>
> You would also like to be the church approached for a photo to run with another particular news story.

Advertising Consultants

You will be approached throughout the year by various advertising consultants / executives (sales people) from the various newspaper publishers inviting you to advertise. They may have an upcoming feature, special for main body advert, or a place for a 'stressed advert (see below)'.

If you have a plan (CMP), of which they are aware, then these approaches will be less frequent. It is best to advise your consultant at the start of the year about your advertising plans for their publication.

If you have no plan advised to them and you just place adverts across the publication without any particular plan, you will find that the consultant more likely thinks that you are a chance at any number of placements throughout the year. You will quite possibly be regularly approached.

'Stressed advert'

This is a system whereby the newspaper consultant needs to fill a space urgently either because it hasn't sold or there has been an unforeseen withdrawal.

It is often a good idea to advise your consultant that you are willing to use their 'stressed' advertising system.

Having a good friendly relationship with your advertising consultant, who is usually developed over the phone, often helps. This, along with your account size, is a key factor.

> The most important aspects they consider will be your ability to produce an advert in a short time with little notification, along with your ability to pay.

> **Stressed adverts are often considerably cheaper and at bargain prices!**

Depending on their desperation and the size of your account with them, you may even negotiate the price.

S/he will give you up to a day usually, sometimes just a few hours, to create your own advertisement or get their graphic artists everything they need to create one for you.

> **The best plan for this type of advertising is to have advertisements already prepared or repeat a good advert already published by that outlet.**
>
> **You may also have all the details and pics (photographs) ready to be sent.**

You will also need various sized adverts as you never know the space size to be filled.

Magazine Advertising Overview

Magazine advertising is similar to newspaper advertising, yet the costs are usually higher.

However, a full page is considerably smaller than a newspaper's.

You need to find the best magazine which suits your parish's philosophy and will accept advertisements in your price bracket.

Local magazines are often the best for parishes - better target audience and less expensive.

Magazines are usually of a better print, paper and presentation quality as compared to newspapers.

> Magazines usually lie around homes and offices longer than newspapers and hence have a longer lasting church marketing value.

Creating a magazine advertisement is similar to that of newspapers.

Creating the Newspaper and Magazine Advertisement - Instructions

Be prepared! Be creative! Do not rush!

Overall Tips

When creating a newspaper or magazine advertisement it is suggested that you:

- Use the Church branding style.

- Be succinct and make sure the advert is not too busy (crowded with content and photos).

- Allow for the advert size impacting on how much should be included.

- Be brief. Brevity is best! A clean appearance is striking!

- Have a layout which attracts the eye of the reader, instantaneously.

- Use good photos. Relevant, striking and of a high quality in appearance.

- Use advice where necessary. Another valued opinion is often worthwhile!

Depending on the time of the year, you will need to use the theme decided upon according to your CMP - unless the plan needs updating due to changed circumstances.

Decide who will create the finished product – your parish or the newspaper / magazine publisher's graphic artists.

The Plan - Instructions

- **Collect Resources:**

  * the pic/s needed
  * church logo
  * parish catch-phrase / motto
  * branding graphics
  * branding style
  * branding colors
  * church name in branded style
  * text for the advert
  * contact details and layout

- **Creative Decisions:**

  * Layout placement overall of each individual item according to branding style

  * Layout of advertising text e.g. sentence form or note form and placement

  * Relative font sizes and font styles of each section

  * Direction photos facing – photos should look into the page and not off the page i.e. people and structures etc face into the page (This draws the reader into the gist of the page.)

  * Background colors, according to branding

  * Use the advertisement size to decide – be succinct and non-busy

- **Create the Advertisement (according to the above):**

  * If you are fortunate enough to have a graphic artist or someone with a good knowledge of publishing software on the parish staff or as a parishioner this would be highly beneficial. You may sit with, or give a briefing to, this person who needs to be fully informed of the branding style and your advertising expectations, or

  * If you decide the publication's graphic artist will create the advertisement, you will need to send all the details plus layout design (at least a sketch) you have decided. You may give them some freedom; however make sure they are aware of the church's branding style.

Directions and Resources to Graphic Artist

> • You will need to be very clear with your directions and resources presented to the graphic artist and prepared to explain these further.

- Be well prepared and accurate in your advice and resources.

- Send everything needed to the graphic artist **in one go**!

- It is not a good idea to send something later as it is very annoying to the graphic artist and could also be misplaced or misunderstood.

- A good method is to email the text and photos along with a sketched layout to either your graphic artist or the publisher's. Emailing is another popular possibility. You may have to send the sketch on 'Paint' software or the like.

- You could also present a previous advert as the general layout required and then add / show any changes.

- Have the first proof done and then evaluate. Get other opinions, if desired.

- Have necessary changes made. Evaluate the next proof. Have minor changes made. Evaluate the final proof. This should complete the process.

- You have every right to get this correct. Accuracy of branding and spelling is critical.

- When happy with the final product, the PMM should make the final call and sign-off.

Radio Advertising

It's COOL!

Radio Advertising is considered by a major component of the community as being 'COOL'!

And effective!

Especially in the <45 demographic.

This could be quite effective for churches with a unique angle!

For many churches this would be a foreign form of advertising.

As with most marketing –
being one of the first to use this form in your community could work well in your favor.

The cutting edge approach is usually beneficial!

Cost is Relatively Expensive – Worth Considering

This is a relatively expensive form of advertising, but one which appears to be quite successful if done correctly and on the right radio station.

Often the expense is worth the overall results.

The expense occurs due to the nature of having a series of advertisements run over a period e.g. 2-3 weeks. I believe that this is the ideal time for a campaign.

Individual adverts and 'live reads' are reasonable in price.

'Live reads' are partially scripted reads with a live feel, done as a discussion if two announcers are present. These sound to the listener as if the station / announcers are endorsing the church – very effective but more expensive.

These could be pre-recorded or done live.

Positives are Potentially Numerous:

> - the awareness developed in the listening public of the place of your church within the community and special characteristics the church offers

- the interest gained in a number of people to visit and hopefully more fully engage in the parish

- the interest gained to at least look at your church in more detail with the possibility of engaging more permanently at a later date

- the 'coolness' factor built up within your own community

- the 'coolness' factor developed within the general public.

> Your community gains a positive sense of the church's wellbeing and place within your city / town.

Basically, it is seen as cool to go to your church.

Campaign Enhancements

The radio campaign will often include other aspects to enhance the campaign. These could include:

- attendance by the station personnel at a special event

- live-crosses to their mobile vans in the field mentioning your special event

- being at the event and advertising through live-crosses

- for a significant further charge the station could do a whole live broadcast of one of their shows from your parish. For example, if there was a Parish Open Day in the afternoon, the morning radio show could be broadcast live from the front of your church to promote the Open Day. This could also include fun activities for children e.g. games and prizes, plus promotional banners, large PA, etc. This is very effective but also expensive

Advertising by Parish, Cluster or Deanery?

Radio advertising by an individual parish is possibly best for a parish in a non-capital city due to cost and relevance. (Is an advertised parish in an outer suburb of a capital city relevant to a person on the other side of town?)

However, if done through a cluster of similar or localized parishes or deanery, it could also be successful in a capital city. The parishes may be based geographically e.g. bayside or country parishes.

> For clusters or deanery, promoting a few positives of some of the churches, often has a roll-on effect for the other churches to also be perceived positively.

Being too specific e.g. for certain order parishes, could be of a disadvantage due to its minimal appeal resulting from smaller cluster.

Audience Demographic

The radio station would need to have your target audience as its main target demographic. For young families with children up to high school age a successful demographic would be women in the 25 to 45 age bracket.

Mothers usually have the major say in selecting their parish (or in fact whether to attend or not).

Advertising Times

A successful program of advertisements on commercial radio station would normally run over a two to three week period. A concentrated two week period may also be successful.

The radio slots would need to be in the play brackets which suit your targeted demographic. The best times are often breakfast and drive-home times. The next session for mothers is usually the morning session.

Suitability of Stations

Be careful of radio stations which play large groups of adverts in each advert block. Your advert could possibly get lost amongst the busyness of these blocks of adverts.

Not every station would be suitable for your parish e.g. some stations have an amount of inappropriate discussion or inappropriate advertisements occurring and are recognized this way within society.

If you get tied up through paid advertising with these stations, your reputation would more than likely be adversely affected.

Be Prepared

Be prepared and organized well before your marketing period e.g. if wanting radio advertising to run in December for Christmas have contract and advertisement slot sessions signed and sealed no later than June; preferably by February or even by the end of the year before to get advert time slots.

Good stations usually fill their slots many months in advance.

If you leave making a decision on which proposal to accept too close to your marketing period, be aware that the consultant may have difficulty booking advert times in the sessions you require.

It may also impact on pre-recording of advert and 'live' read times.

Advertising Consultants and Proposals Plan

- Initially make contact with selected radio stations and speak with their marketing / advertising people regarding a possible radio marketing plan.

- If you don't make contact, then more than likely the radio station's advertising or marketing consultants will contact the church's CMM and request an interview to discuss a possible radio marketing plan.

- Gain proposals from 2-3 stations you would be happy to have advertise your church. These may also be based on the stations which other parishes use or you feel suit your target audience.

- At the interview have a basic budget figure so that a realistic plan can be offered to you.

- If you do not want to give the figure at this stage of the negotiations you may like to give a range you are prepared to consider. (Probably allowing for a little leeway for the upper figure in later negations.)

- You do not have to accept the proposals.

> - **This is a good time to negotiate the number of ads, placement times and cost. There is usually some leeway from the station at this time. The consultant will usually be able to include extra slots 'free of charge' or change some slots to better times. Sometimes the overall cost may be reduced.**

- Be professional in all negotiations and realize that there is a bottom line for the station, just as there is for your school.

- Once everything is agreed the CMM will have to sign a contract on behalf of the church to accept the proposal.

- The CMM often needs to discuss any proposal and cost with the Parish Priest / Pastor. This is a relatively large financial commitment as part of the Church Marketing Budget.

Special Event Day

A radio campaign often includes the station's attendance at a special event e.g. the Parish Open Day or Fete.

The station sets up their flags and banners etc.

They will often have one of their vans / cars / trucks in attendance. This has their logo and colors brightly displayed. (It is often considered 'cool' by many adults and children alike to be linked with a cool radio station.)

These all helps to develop a party / fun atmosphere.

There will normally be live crosses to the van personality throughout the week promoting the special event. These live crosses are often more effective if there is a continuation through the special event day.

This is often seen as very 'cool' by many people in attendance - especially the school communities. Once again this helps to develop the support of one of the key stakeholders, the school communities.

Remember that the best marketers a parish has are their own parishioners.

Creating a Radio Advertisement + Instructions + Sample

Overview for Success

> The script and script reader/s are two of the most important aspects when creating the radio advertisement.

> You will most likely need to use the **creative department** of the radio station to write the scripts – after presenting your basic required text.
>
> Their expertise is in 'radio talk' and how to get a message across in an inspirational way and with the minimum of words.

Most adverts are 30-45 seconds in length.

You may like the occasional 60 second advert for variety.

Costs vary according to length and often the time slot played in.

Standard adverts are recorded in the studio prior to transmission.

'Live-reads' have a major impact on the listener. Costs for these are much higher than a recorded advert.

> Best to have specific themes and not to just have advertisements telling the public how good the church is.
>
> Without themes it may appear as desperation by the parish to attract parishioners.

A three week campaign will normally have 2-3 themes, often one per week e.g.:

- Week 1 – Advent events
- Week 2 – Christmas celebrations
- Week 3 – New Year: looking to the future year...

This then appears as if the parish is open to people seeing how good it is and what it has to offer, with the possibility of engagement for interested new parishioners.

Scripts

The advertising consultant will usually request from the CMM the points you wish covered in both the adverts and the live-reads. If not, you will need to take the initiative – they probably don't your church or what you want highlighted.

Try to be clear and succinct and not to include too much detail. The creative people will use brevity and clarity in producing their scripts.

> You may like to try doing 30-45 second advertisements yourself to see how many words suit.
> Remember to use 'radio talk' – inflections, etc.

Once these are written by the station (See below for an example) they will normally be emailed to the CMM for proofing. Proof these and advise them of any changes, but be realistic.

> The scripts will often appear to be too brief and you will want to add more.
>
> Be aware that a 30 second read isn't really much.
> Your best action would be to adjust what is there.
>
> Realistically, if you wish to add something you will probably have to delete something else.

Reader/s Voice

The reader/s is an extremely important aspect of the advert and needs to be decided well.

A suggestion of the people you may get to record your scripts for you:

- A personality recognized by the listeners. This could be expensive unless the personality is a parishioner or staff member, etc.

- Key people from within the parish:

    * This could include from the schools. A School Captain is usually a good choice to appeal to the younger members of your community (providing they have the skills).

    * Another easily recognized parishioner or parish staff member who has the necessary credentials and would be appreciated by the target audience e.g. with major business, cultural or sporting success, or who has a special reason for coming to your parish.

- A key recognizable person from within the deanery or diocese.

- Generic people the station employ. These come at a cost, usually anywhere from a couple of hundred dollars in non-capital cities, to often more than double this in capitals.

Recordings – CMM Role

A time will be arranged for whoever is decided by the CMM to record the adverts at the station. This should be an enjoyable time for all concerned.

It is a good idea for the CMM to be in attendance to make sure the recording is as expected.
The CMM needs to be a calming influence.

Minor script or voice inflection adjustments are possible.

If students or young people are involved the CMM, or well informed designate, in most, if not all cases, must attend. This is both for support and duty of care.

A calm CMM is necessary for an effective performance by the readers.

Radio stations should send you, usually by email, the completed agreed-to recorded adverts for your perusal and records.

Check that these are the recordings to be used.

If these are not the agreed to recordings, or include elements not requested or required, immediately contact your consultant and arrange for adjustments before the advert goes to air.

Recording Cautions

The CMM, or informed designate, should be present during all recordings. This also allows for any inappropriate comments or misunderstandings to be rectified before going to air.

This becomes more apparent for the recording of 'live reads' when announcers have a banter going with each other and maybe your young people.

Live Reads and Other Cautions

However, you have little control over unrecorded 'live reads' apart from agreeing to the initial key points / 'script'.

If these are treated inappropriately by the radio announcers when going to air, you will need to contact your advertising consultant immediately and have the situation resolved.

This would usually involve extra adverts, on-air apologies, etc depending on the severity of the inappropriateness.

Rarely an unapproved advertisement gets played. If this does happen, make immediate contact with the Consultant and have the advertisement 'pulled' and replaced or rectified. Negotiated benefits to the parish could occur also.

These errors on the part of the station would often see them offering to place a few more ads as compensation for you and for their good name not to be tarnished. Initially leave this offer up to them to make. If it isn't made then make contact and request some form of compensation.

Recordings for Church Community / Website / On-Hold

The recordings can also be emailed to all parishioners, and anyone else on your email lists.

Most people enjoy downloading these and sharing with family and friends – an indirect form of marketing, but usually a successful one.

Placement on the parish's website is also a major advantage.

These are also good for your marketing records or for playing to selected audiences e.g. Parish Pastoral Council and Board meetings.

> The parish telephone's 'On-Hold' recording could often be a successful radio advert recording.

Copyright

> Copyright – You need to obtain the radio station's permission first, if you do not own the copyright, to avoid any possible copyright infringements.

Campaign Advertisement Play Time

The radio station should send the times for each day's advertising slots prior to each day. This usually happens the day before.

If this doesn't happen it will need to be followed up. These lists help you check that you are getting what you ordered. As you will not be available for all slots, try and have others also listen and report back to you.

You are also able to advise your community of the times for them to listen.

The live reads should be good presentations and effective to your campaign.

SAMPLE Follows.........

Various details have been removed to protect student identities.

LIVE READ SCRIPT:

102.9 fm
hot tomato

Client:	
Product:	Live Read (Pre recorded interview)
Length:	29

Date written:	
Acc Mgr:	AL
Writer:	KH

Start Date:		End Date:	
Key No:	AQUCOL140507LIVE	Cart:	2313

DAY:_____

TIME: _____

Script outline only**. *Luke and Flan to record two versions each (Luke will need an extra tag)*

Luke / Flan: [Captains' Names] from Aquinas College are here with me... because Aquinas College has got an open day from 2 to 5 this Friday... and you guys are out pressing the flesh!

Captain 1: That's right!

Captain 2: Sure am.

Luke: So tell me, what's so good about Aquinas...?

Captain 1: It's friendly, supportive. It's a great place to be yourself, an individual!

Captain 2: It's got IT centres, fully equipped laboratories, art and drama centres... everything you could want.

Captain 1: Whether you want to go to uni, or do a trade, Aquinas will show you how to do it... and the teachers are right behind you all the way.

Luke / Flan: Sounds like it does pretty well for a school!

Captain 2: Oh yeah... it's way more than a school!

Luke / Flan: The Aquinas College Open Day – this Friday from 2 till 5. Go see for yourself why these guys say, Aquinas is more than just a school!

(Source 102.9 Hot Tomato, Gold Coast)

Television Advertising

"It's cool!" Even more cool than radio - A commonly held view by many of the church community.

Television advertising is an expensive form of advertising.

It is difficult to justify the expense / success ratio!

Television is most likely seen as the coolest main line commercial medium.

Beware: the challenges!

- **Quality**

Television advertising is fraught with various levels of the 'cringe factor' if not produced and presented in a very professional manner. Quality is paramount, as all weaknesses are multiplied when shown on air.

- **Large Cities**

Capital city advertising is very expensive. Similar to radio, there remains the question as to whether there is any benefit in advertising over a large area for a specific parish or church in one location.

Deanery or diocesan advertising would often be of benefit for those churches within the region. There is also the flow-on effect of like parishes e.g. other Catholic parishes being seen as equivalent to the advertised ones.

- **Smaller Cities and Towns**

Smaller cities and towns also have the question mark over the effectiveness of this form of advertising against the cost involved. Quality of production may also be questionable.

The local television channels usually only produce a nightly news program. All other shows are normally direct feeds from the main networks. The advertising is added from the local station and interspersed with the major companies' adverts.

> The major question here is, how many people watch the local station when they could be watching the main networked station in most cases?
>
> Hence, how successful would placing local adverts through the local station be?

Television Station Advertising List – Learn from...

- **The best way to decide on this is to see the local channel's list of advertisers.**

This is easily obtained from the station's advertising consultants. Once you have the list, check the businesses, parishes, schools and community groups etc which advertise.

- **Does this list inspire you to also advertise with this channel?**

It may become apparent that no really significant local or larger business accounts exist and hence there is probably little reason for you to use this form.

If the major businesses and community groups don't use it there is usually a good reason why. This reason is most likely that the number of viewers is limited.

> A case could be made for regional or diocesan advertising in these smaller places.
>
> Once again, check who are the present advertisers and decide whether this suits your CMP.

Creating a Television Advertisement

The proposal

> You will usually need to work closely with either the television creative department of the station you select, or an advertising agency, to develop a professionally produced advertisement.

Professional Quote / Presentation Proposal

A good practice is to get quotes for costs along with a proposal for what each group can offer you.

A professional group will put together a proposal which would include a DVD / website downloads, etc of successful advertisements they have created, or advertising styles they could use.

The CMM or other key staff member / designate will need to devote considerable time to this venture.

The Parish Priest or Pastor, in most cases, needs to be involved with most of these processes.

It is often best for the CMM to plan with the Parish Priest / Pastor early on the involvement s/he would like and how best to meet these requirements.

> Just as with the church's DVD production, it is a wonderful marketing strategy to include the fact that the church has a TV advertisement, plus excerpts from the final advertisement's production, in various components of the CMP.

You can always use the rider "As seen on television…" in various marketing endeavors.

CMM and Advertisement Preparations

Working in conjunction with the selected artistic group, you will more than likely need to assist the production preparation through helping to:

- develop scripts
- select and arrange scenes and props
- select actors
- develop a shooting schedule, which allows for the unexpected e.g. rain
- oversee rehearsals

The CMM or talented and fully informed staff member / parishioner / parish consultant should take an active role in the whole preparation process to help achieve the desired product.

Include Your Parish Personnel and Facilities

The parish should be involved as much as possible in the production.

> The scenes should mostly be settings from the church or parish for authenticity. This helps the parish be seen in a good light within the parish community and the viewing public.

Using outside studios can give the wrong impression. It also takes away the opportunity of claiming the advert shows only your parish when using other marketing forms.

Other key people and their roles within the parish may be involved at different stages.

These people could include:

- Parish Priest or Pastor, overall, as well as if being interviewed or recorded as part of a scene/s
- Parish Staff
- Parishioners
- Staff from your schools, including:

    * Drama staff for casting / acting
    * Music staff for background music
    * Art and Industrial Skills staff for settings and props
    * IT and Film and Television staff for graphics and some production involvement
    * Other departments for classroom scenes
    * Students either as lead roles or in various scenes.

The CMM's Role in Production

The CMM will most likely need to:

- Oversee most aspects of the production – be Producer or Co-Producer
- Be present at all videoing times
- View the various rushes / videoed scenes to make sure these fit the desired outcome
- Work with music people to help create appropriate background music which aligns with the finished production
- Work with graphics people to obtained desired graphics
- Work within the budget and not place expectations which may have a negative impact on the budget
- Work with post-production to assist with final editing

The CMM will usually need to tread a fine line between being of assistance to the production and of being an unhelpful intrusion.

> The CMM, or designate, needs to use the skills of the experts, yet keep everyone on task to achieve the previously decided outcome.

It is best, at times, to back off if being a diplomat is difficult or not possible in some situations.

Gaining assistance from another source e.g. Parish Priest or the diocesan Communications and Marketing Manager can often help in these situations.

Church Marketing Action Plan

Time to use the church marketing plan to begin your Action Plan.

Follow the plan over the next few activity pages.
You may need to do some research before beginning to select the various strategies with which you might like to begin.
Use the samples, suggestions and instructions included in the e-book to assist.

Work within your budget. Good things grow from successes.
Remember - the better the planning, the better the result!

Define what you have to offer:

- vision and mission, personnel, sacramental / prayer life, pastoral and welfare support programs, schools, religious and pastoral education, facilities, etc

- specific ages and groups catered for - from infants to the elderly

- future plans – programs, staffing, facilities, etc

Define your target group:

- through surveys, observations, experience, gifts and talents available / needed

- proximity to / involvement with church educational institutes – elementary / primary, secondary and tertiary

- any expansion – programs, facilities, staffing

Budget:

- realistically support the church marketing plan

- be flexible and open to growth and change as the needs arise

- continually develop over time through needs and experiences

Personnel and talents available - including Church Marketing Manager

Select Marketing Strategies:

- Church Marketing Relationships

- Church Marketing Resources (including branding, advertising)

- Using the Media

  * Internet and other Contemporary methods

  * Both for Free (Media Releases / Editorial, etc) and for Fee (Advertising) Evaluation

Evaluation

Church Marketing Action Plan

Define what you have to offer:

- vision and mission, personnel, sacramental / prayer life, pastoral and welfare support programs, schools, religious and pastoral education, facilities, etc

Church Marketing Action Plan

Define what you have to offer:

- specific ages and groups catered for - from infants to the elderly

Church Marketing Action Plan

Define what you have to offer:

- future plans – programs, staffing, facilities, etc

Church Marketing Action Plan

Define your target group:

- through surveys, observations, experience, gifts and talents available / needed

Church Marketing Action Plan

Define your target group:

- proximity to / involvement with church educational institutes – elementary / primary, secondary and tertiary

Church Marketing Action Plan

Define your target group:

- any expansion – programs, facilities, staffing

Church Marketing Action Plan

Budget:

- realistically support the church marketing plan

- be flexible and open to growth and change as the needs arise

- continually develop over time through needs and experiences

Church Marketing Action Plan

Personnel and talents available - including Church Marketing Manager

Church Marketing Action Plan

Select Marketing Strategies:

- **Church Marketing Relationships**

Church Marketing Action Plan

Select Marketing Strategies:

- **Church Marketing Resources (including branding, advertising)**

Church Marketing Action Plan

Select Marketing Strategies:

- **Use the Media**

    * **Internet and other Contemporary methods**

    * **Both for Free (Media Releases / Editorial, etc) and for Fee (Advertising)**

Church Marketing Action Plan

Evaluation

Conclusion

The journey to successfully market your church is a challenging and hopefully rewarding one for all involved. The main challenge is to be well informed, well prepared and to execute well.

Keeping informed of best practice is critical.

Know what your Church Marketing Plan requires. Appreciate all its components and intricacies. Be aware of important resources and be prepared to attend professional development courses.

I believe that this book is one such resource developed as a result of almost two decades of marketing within the Church. Another good resource is the interactive website at: http://.churchparishmarketing.com . These sorts of managed interactive websites will play a key role in the future for church marketing.

I invite you to continue the engagement begun with me through the *Church Marketing Manual for the Digital Age* (2nd ed) and the previous *Church Parish Marketing e-Handbook: Easy to Use Guide to Market Your Church Parish Deanery* into the world of the future through this Church Parish Marketing (CPM) website.

I began this book with the challenge to you to develop an effective, efficient and creative Church Marketing Plan. I invited you to engage with what the text offers through three steps:

- Initially to explore a Sample OVERVIEW of a Church Marketing Plan.

- Next to study the detail throughout this Manual to gain an intimate knowledge of the 'what, why and how' of the requirements for a successful church marketing plan.

- Finally to begin your own **Church Marketing Action Plan**.

May I offer you all the best with developing your Action Plan.

Your feedback is always much appreciated.

Thought - Detailed Brevity, Creativity and Experience are important keys to the puzzle!

**The future awaits … don't let an opportunity go! The Church can not afford it!
My prayers are with you.**

Glossary

Ad or Advert	advertisement
Busy	the overall layout has too much detail and will not encourage further exploration
Copy	text
Live-reads	radio adverts which sound to the listener as a discussion or statement by the on-air announcer/s and hence have more credibility; follow a basic script but allow for improvisation
Looped	a visual or audio recording that is set to automatically repeat indefinitely each time it is played completely
Pics	photos
Proof	a draft
Slots	radio specific times for radio or television advertising
Stressed adverts	form of advertising whereby little notification by newspaper outlet is given for advert creation and placement but at a considerably reduced cost rate
CMP	Church Marketing Plan
CMB	Church Marketing Budget
CMM	Church Marketing Manager
CMR	Church Marketing Resources
SMM	School Marketing Manager
DMP	Deanery Marketing Plan

Bibliography

Websites used, or referred to, in this Book.

All websites below were viewed in January, 2010.

http://au.yahoo.com/

http://blog.whitepages.com/2009/01/29/free-text-messaging-from-your-computer/

http://bne.catholic.net.au/asp/index.asp

http://churchparishmarketing.com/

http://churchparishmarketing.com/_blog/Church_Marketing_Blog

http://churchparishmarketing.com/_blog/Church_Marketing_Blog/post/Give_some_love_and_forgiveness/

http://churchparishmarketing.com/_blog/Church_Marketing_Blog/post/Mary_MacKillop_-_Australia's_First_Saint/

http://churchparishmarketing.com/_catalog_29976/Books

http://churchparishmarketing.com/_webapp_273892/Family_Moments

http://churchparishmarketing.com/blog-conditions-of-use

http://churchparishmarketing.com/bryan_foster

http://churchparishmarketing.com/contact-us

http://churchparishmarketing.com/e-handbook

http://churchparishmarketing.com/gallery

http://churchparishmarketing.com/hints-tips

http://churchparishmarketing.com/news

http://churchparishmarketing.com/RSSRetrieve.aspx?ID=4441&Type=RSS20

http://churchparishmarketing.com/specials

http://churchparishmarketing.com/sponsorship

http://churchparishmarketing.com/testimonials

http://churchparishmarketing.com/videos

http://cid-be3b1afd17150174.profile.live.com/details/editname.aspx?ru=http://cid-be-3b1afd17150174.profile.live.com/details/EditPsm.aspx

http://cidbe3b1afd17150174.profile.live.com/details/editprofileaccess.aspx?pa=psm&ru=http%3a%2f%2fcid-be3b1afd17150174.profile.live.com%2fdetails%2fEditPsm.aspx

http://cidbe3b1afd17150174.profile.live.com/details/editpsm.aspx?ru=http%3a%2f%2fhome.live.com%2f&sa=590590424

http://download.live.com/

http://download.live.com/messenger

http://en.wikipedia.org/wiki/List_of_social_networking_websites

http://en.wordpress.com/signup/

http://europe.nokia.com/support/download-software/nokia-ovi-suite/howto/manage-your-text-messages/send-and-receive-text-messages

http://faq.myspace.com/app/

http://help.live.com//help.aspx?project=WL_Profile&market=en-AU&querytype=keyword&query=yrogetac&tmt=&domain=cid-be3b1afd17150174.profile.live.com&format=b1

http://help.live.com//help.aspx?project=WL_Profile&market=enAU&querytype=keyword&query=yrogetac&tmt=&domain=cid-be3b1afd17150174.profile.live.com&format=b1

http://help.live.com/help.aspx?project=tou&mkt=en-us

http://home.live.com/

http://login.live.com/login.srf?wa=wsignin1.0&rpsnv=11&ct=1263351950&rver=6.0.5285.0&wp=MBI&wreply=http:%2F%2Fmail.live.com%2Fdefault.aspx&lc=1033&id=64855&mkt=en-au

http://mail.live.com/?rru=inbox

http://mail.live.com/mail/about.aspx

http://meaning-of-life-is-love.blogspot.com/

http://meaning-of-life-is-love.blogspot.com/2010/01/give-little-forgiveness-and-love.html

http://meaningoflifeislove.wordpress.com/

http://meaningoflifeislove.wordpress.com/2010/01/12/love-and-forgiveness/

http://privacy.microsoft.com/en-au/default.mspx

http://schoolmarketingehandbook.com/

http://scp.org.au/

http://signups.myspace.com/index.cfm?fuseaction=signup

http://smallbusiness.yahoo.com/

http://store.apple.com/us/product/MB278Z/A?fnode=MTY1NDAzOA&mco=MTA4MjgwODY

http://store.apple.com/us/product/MB642Z/A?fnode=MTY1NDAzOA&mco=MTA4MjgwNzk

http://store.apple.com/us/product/MB966Z/A/iLife09?fnode=MTY1NDAzOA&mco=MTM3NDc5MjU

http://tweeternet.com/#tools

http://twitter.com/

http://twitter.com/about

http://twitter.com/aquinasrulz

http://twitter.com/home

http://twitter.com/privacy

http://twittgroups.com/confirm.php?oauth_token=d5G5hhEuJGJVY6cwtZjO9sMuqUtch
AUfGtoLzTdltDs

http://twittgroups.com/index.php

http://upload.youtube.com/my_videos_upload

http://wordpress.com/

http://www.adobe.com/products/premiere/

http://www.adobe.com/products/premiere/

http://www.adobe.com/products/premiereel/

http://www.alwaysinteractive.com/

http://www.alwaysinteractive.com/iceberg/quicktour/

http://www.alwaysinteractive.com/iceberg/video/

http://www.basic-digital-photography.com/shooting-photos.html

http://www.bbc.co.uk/arts/apictureofbritain/how_to/

http://www.blogger.com/choose-template-new.g?blogID=5084059280509222521

http://www.blogger.com/create-blog.g?pli=1

http://www.blogger.com/start

http://www.choice.com.au/Reviews-and-Tests/Technology/Cameras-and-camcorders/
Digital-cameras/Digital-SLR-cameras-review-and-compare/Page/Introduction.aspx

http://www.corel.com/servlet/Satellite/us/en/Product/1175714228541#tabview=tab0

http://www.crestock.com/

http://www.cyberlink.com/products/powerdirector/overview_en_US.html

http://www.dailymotion.com/en

http://www.dailymotion.com/register

http://www.facebook.com/

http://www.facebook.com/adrian.sharp2?ref=ts

http://www.facebook.com/group.php?gid=146341449337

http://www.facebook.com/group.php?gid=14891935948&ref=search&sid=1418024383.3181693141..1

http://www.facebook.com/group.php?gid=14891935948&ref=search&sid=100000138432659.2074770501..1#/group.php?v=wall&ref=search&gid=14891935948

http://www.facebook.com/group.php?gid=14891935948&ref=search&sid=1418024383.3181693141..1

http://www.facebook.com/group.php?v=wall&ref=search&gid=14891935948

http://www.facebook.com/help/

http://www.facebook.com/help/#/help/?page=420

http://www.facebook.com/help/#/help/?page=439

http://www.facebook.com/help/#/help/?page=440

http://twitter.com/oauth/authorize?oauth_token=d5G5hhEuJGJVY6cwtZjO9sMuqUtchAUfGtoLzTdltDs

http://www.facebook.com/help/#/help/?page=756

http://www.facebook.com/help/?page=419

http://www.facebook.com/index.php?lh=d13e2bf3830acecd51754253db99a7eb&

http://www.facebook.com/pages/Love-is-the-Meaning-of-Life/265813695571

http://www.facebook.com/pages/Love-is-the-Meaning-of-Life/265813695571?created

http://www.facebook.com/reqs.php

http://www.facebook.com/twitter/?redirect=265813695571

http://www.facebook.com/twitter/?redirect=276454385999#

http://www.facebook.com/twitter/?redirect=276454385999#/pages/Meaning-of-Life-is-Love/276454385999

http://www.flickr.com/

http://www.flickr.com/photos/upload/

http://www.google.com/support/youtube/bin/answer.py?answer=132460&topic=16612&hl=en-US

http://www.gowindowslive.com/hotmailplus/en-au/default.aspx

http://www.istockphoto.com/index.php

http://www.joomla.org/

http://www.kodak.com/eknec/PageQuerier.jhtml?pq-path=317&pq-locale=en_AU&requestid=42257

http://www.linkedin.com/

http://www.linkedin.com/createGroup?displayCreate=&trk=anet_creategrp

http://www.linkedin.com/groupAnswers?viewQuestions=&gid=2242194&forumID=3&sik=1264051915108

http://www.linkedin.com/home?trk=hb_home

http://www.linkedin.com/myprofile?trk=hb_tab_pro

http://www.linkedin.com/static?key=privacy_policy

http://www.linkedin.com/static?key=user_agreement

http://www.microsoft.com/technet/security/bulletin/secrssinfo.mspx

http://www.movabletype.org/

http://www.myspace.com/

http://www.myspace.com/bryanfoster1

http://www.plaxo.com/

http://www.plaxo.com/signup?page=2

http://www.schoolmarketingaustralia.com/

http://www.schoolmarketingaustralia.com/_blog/School_Marketing_Blog

http://www.schoolzine.com.au/

http://www.skype.com/

http://www.skype.com/intl/en/allfeatures/videocall/

http://www.skype.com/intl/en/download/skype/windows/

http://www.skype.com/intl/en/legal/

http://www.telstra.com.au/mobile/services/messaging/online_text_buddy.html

http://www.tumblr.com/

http://www.typepad.com/pro/#2

http://www.vox.com/

http://www.windowslive-hotmail.com/LearnMore/

http://www.youtube.com/

http://www.youtube.com/create_account

http://www.youtube.com/create_account?next=%2F

http://www.youtube.com/watch?v=LHKcGUlhdlc

https://edit.yahoo.com/registration?.intl=au&domain=y7mail.com&.src=ym&.done=http://au.mail.yahoo.com

https://signup.live.com/signup.aspx?ru=http%3a%2f%2fmail.live.com%2f%3frru%3dinbox&wa=wsignin1.0&rpsnv=11&ct=1263351950&rver=6.0.5285.0&wp=MBI&wreply=http:%2F%2Fmail.live.com%2Fdefault.aspx&lc=1033&id=64855&mkt=en-au&bk=1263351951&rollrs=12&lic=1

https://signup.live.com/signup.aspx?ru=http%3a%2f%2fmail.live.com%2f%3frru%3dinbox&wa=wsignin1.0&rpsnv=11&ct=1263351950&rver=6.0.5285.0&wp=MBI&wreply=http:%2F%2Fmail.live.com%2Fdefault.aspx&lc=1033&id=64855&mkt=en-au&bk=1263351951&rollrs=12&lic=1

https://twitter.com/oauth/authorize?oauth_token=w7vv0SUaJzN5xAseicYUCXphnvZ9xpfKJIA5ePeyrXo

https://twitter.com/signup

https://www.blogger.com/start

https://www.google.com/accounts/NewAccount?service=blogger&continue=https%3A%2F%2Fwww.blogger.com%2Floginz%3Fd%3D%252Fcreate-blog.g%26a%3DADD_SER-

VICE_FLAG&hl=en&sendvemail=true&followup=https%3A%2F%2Fwww.blogger.com%2Fl oginz%3Fd%3D%252Fhome%26a%3DSERVICE_ONLY&naui=8

https://www.google.com/accounts/ServiceLogin?service=mail&passive=true&rm=false &continue=https%3A%2F%2Fmail.google.com%2Fmail%2F%3Fui%3Dhtml%26zy%3Dl&bsv =zpwhtygjntrz&ss=1&scc=1&ltmpl=default&ltmplcache=2&hl=en

http://www.1029hottomato.com.au/why-radio-works.aspx

www.stmarys.com

www.stmarys.net

www.stmarys.org

www.stmaryschurch.org

www.stmarysparish.org

Index

Made in the USA
Lexington, KY
07 March 2013